# LONG DISTANCE

## TESTING THE LIMITS OF BODY AND SPIRIT
## IN A YEAR OF LIVING STRENUOUSLY

D0026952

# BILL McKIBBEN

RODALE

Rodale books may be purchased for business or promotional use or for special sales. For information, please write to:
Special Markets Department, Rodale, Inc., 733 Third Avenue, New York, NY 10017

Printed in the United States of America
Rodale Inc. makes every effort to use acid-free ♾, recycled paper ♻.

Book design by Christopher Rhoads

First published in hardcover by Simon & Schuster in 2000 and in paperback by Plume in 2001. This paperback edition, with a new introduction, is published by Rodale Inc. in 2010.


Library of Congress Cataloging-in-Publication Data

McKibben, Bill.
    Long distance : testing the limits of body and spirit in a year of living strenuously / Bill McKibben.
        p.    cm.
    ISBN-13 978–1–60529–124–6    paperback
    1. Cross-country ski racing. 2. Cross-country ski racing—Training. 3. McKibben, Bill. I. Title.
GV855.5.R33M35 2010
796.93'2—dc22                                                            2010021734

Distributed to the trade by Macmillan
2   4   6   8   10   9   7   5   3   1   paperback

LIVE YOUR WHOLE LIFE™

We inspire and enable people to improve their lives and the world around them.

**Also by Bill McKibben**

*Hundred Dollar Holiday*

*Maybe One*

*The Age of Missing Information*

*The End of Nature*

*Hope, Human and Wild*

*The Comforting Whirlwind*

*Enough*

*Deep Economy*

*Fight Global Warming Now*

*Eaarth*

*For Gordon McKibben*

# INTRODUCTION

In the decade since *Long Distance* first came out, the question that other masters athletes have asked me most often is: "You still training?"

And the answer is yes, but. Not like I did in this book—that was a one-year extravaganza, the kind of self-indulgence and solipsism that could be justified by someone in training for an Olympic medal, but not someone trying to come in third in his age group at the local race. Anyway, it wore me right out. By the next year I'd cut my training time in half—to about 300 or 350 hours annually—and that's about where it's stayed ever since. It's still enough to be a major part of my life, but not enough to dominate it, which is good, because I've had other things to do. More important things: watch my daughter grow into a young woman, write a few more books, help organize the largest grassroots climate campaign in the planet's history.

Oddly, cutting back on training didn't really slow me down. Perhaps I'd taken the year described in this book to really jumpstart my body to some new, fit stage—since then, I've been more or less able to maintain that new form. I'm ten years older, but I weigh about the same, and I finish 25 kilometers at about the same pace. And I still love to ski with the same fervor—still lie awake on hot summer nights imagining what the next winter will be like. I'll bike, and I'll run, and I'll paddle, and I'll hike—but it's those frozen months, when friction disappears and a certain kind of grace descends even on the ungainly, that I live for.

I've also had the great good fortune to learn a lot more about racing of all kinds. Ten years ago we moved to Middlebury, Vermont, and I volunteered to be the faculty advisor to the college's Nordic ski team, one of the very best in the country even though all the competition comes from major universities. The team's coaches, Andrew Gardner and Patty Ross, have taught me a whole new depth of appreciation for the sport—and it's been sheer pleasure to get to know dozens of young skiers. This year two of the finest, both as athletes and young men, were on the U.S. Olympic team: it was intriguing to watch Garrott Kuzzy and Simi Hamilton mature into superior athletes over the course of a few seasons.

And a joy as well to see some of the others mentioned in this book come of age. Tim Burke and Lowell Bailey put in brief appearances as teenagers waxing my skis in a Quebec parking lot before my first real race; now they're both Olympic biathletes, and Tim, who is one of the best in the world, is a well-known athletic hero in Europe where they take the sport with NASCAR seriousness.

Some days, usually when the work of trying to fix global warming is going even worse than usual, I find myself thinking that I'd like another yearlong vacation, another chance to live in my body instead of my mind for most of the hours of the day. The sage of a 50-year-old athlete would be different than a 40-year-old—fighting off decay becomes the dominant metaphor at some point. But I'm deeply grateful to have had the chance once, because ever since it's let me watch real athletes and understand their achievements in some deeper way. And it's let me watch my fellow wannabes with great affection. We may not be winning, but we're *winning*.

# 1

I came seeking sweat and found only enlightenment.

It was the first day of January, and I was checking in to the Kripalu Center, a "holistic retreat" in the Berkshire Hills of Massachusetts. I'd come to meet Rob Sleamaker, who had agreed to help turn me into an athlete—to coach me for a year until I was as tough a cross-country ski racer as my genes would allow.

Wandering the halls in search of Rob, who had been hired by Kripalu to teach a weekend course on yoga and skiing, I came across the dining hall, where they were serving butternut squash for supper. "They've put *orange juice* on the squash," said the woman next to me in line, in a tone that implied orange juice was a tangy form of arsenic. I took my tray to the nearest empty chair, which turned out to be next to a man describing craniosacral massage. "You know," he told me in a confidential tone, "if you're generating mucus in one membrane, you're generating it everywhere."

For some reason I ate more quickly than usual and then checked the bulletin board to see if Rob had left a note, but found only posters for upcoming events: "Healing Ourselves/Healing the Planet with Grandmother Rainbow," "The Weeklong Never-Ending Chant," "Living in the Higher Worlds Without Getting Altitude Sickness," "Somatic Explorations of the Jaw." I wandered into a room where a man was orienting first-time visitors. He himself had moved here full-time, he explained, and changed his name to Domadaar. "I want to thank you for coming to share your energies," Domadaar said. "Don't worry about remembering what I'm going to tell you—what's important for you will stick with you, and the rest will dissolve into air." I was beginning to develop a rash. I had come here to jump-start the process of jockification. Forget Grandmother Rainbow; I was looking for Arnold Schwarzenegger. Or so I thought.

Finally I found the room where the cross-country skiing group had gathered. They were sitting cross-legged, listening as a man talked. It must be Rob, whom I'd spoken with on the phone but whom I had never laid eyes on. I'd read his book *Serious Training for Endurance Athletes,* which was filled with lots of graphs of things like "Ventilation and Lactic Acid Changes at the Anaerobic Threshold." The blurbs on the back came from people who, collectively, had won the Ironman triathlon twelve times. And yet as he spoke he sounded sort of like, well, Domadaar. "There's a lot of synergy between yoga and cross-country skiing," he was saying. "You perform so much better when you're relaxed." He glowed with the same sanctified sheen of good health as the other people here.

Happily, though, he proved more than willing to get an unorganic beer in town that night. As we sat, he told me about his life—a boyhood spent playing every possible sport, a degree in exercise physiology from the University of Arizona, a stint working with the U.S. biathlon team. "I started to see the threads of truth that ran through all the various coaching philosophies," he said. "Most of the athletes I knew, their training programs made no sense. Everyone talked about how many miles they'd run, but no one talked about how hard they'd run them." As he warmed to the topic, he took his knife and started drawing a graph on his napkin. "Here's the intensity of your exercise," he said, charting one axis. "Right now, you'd start to get overcome by lactic acid down here, going pretty easy. We want to get you going faster and farther before that buildup starts. *That's what racing is—it's the ability to endure the high production of lactate for a long time.*"

This is more like it, I thought. Enough about the spirit—finally we're getting down to bodies, mine in particular. Finally we're concentrating on what the next twelve months will bring. "After a while you'll get to know your body," Rob said. "After a while it's like getting up in the middle of the night and going to the bathroom—you know where to go. You'll get to the last two kilometers of the race and know that you're not going to bury yourself by going too hard."

But then Rob mentioned in passing that his dad was a preacher, and his granddad too, and just as suddenly the mood shifted. He'd left the church behind, he said, but not an abiding interest in "the process of living." Maybe I rolled my eyes, because he began to speak more quietly and firmly. "Look, life truly is a journey. One of the ways we become whole is to embrace the integration of mind, body, and spirit. If it happens simultaneously, so be it. But we have a whole lifetime. If there is any kind of higher power, I think what it wants is for us to learn as much as we can. You have a mind, you have a body, you have a spirit, and it's important to learn in all three realms. If you want to use just your intellect for one long period, that's okay. But you were born whole, and you can get back to that." Day one of my new life, and already more than I'd bargained for. I had a coach, but I had a guru too, and I was starting to wonder how much difference there was.

For three days our small band skied and stretched; indoors for yoga in the early morning, and then out into the cold. Few in the group had skied before, and since I'd been skiing the woods and lakes of my Adirondack home for a decade, I was the fastest and most fluid. But every once in a while I'd look at Rob or his girlfriend, Carol, who was helping him teach, and be reminded what a real athlete looked like: the economy of motion, the quiet body. Me, I strained constantly, trying to look good. On the last afternoon, I was skiing up a long hill when I noticed Rob behind me. I poured on the coal and powered up the slope, but when I got to the top Rob just said quietly, "You're pushing real hard." I knew that in order to race I'd eventually have to push harder than I'd ever pushed before, but I also knew I was a long way from figuring out the time and the place. For the moment I just relaxed and tried to glide.

That night, after a particularly evolved dinner of something called seitan burgers, I had a dream, one of the few each year I managed to recall. I was the captain of a small tour boat taking sightseers around an improbably compact globe. Though it would have taken just a few minutes to visit the tropics, I kept my boat up north, in the Arctic Ocean. Ice loomed up in great mountains, the winter sun hung low on the horizon, the aurora borealis turned the night sky green and gold. The beauty of this winter was so total it made me tingle while I slept. Omen one.

After I woke up, I came down to breakfast—some new form of soy mush—and read the local paper. A boy from down the road, Patrick Weaver, had just won a spot on the U.S. cross-country team for the upcoming Nagano Olympics, despite a virus that had kept him vomiting throughout the race. "All the time I've been skiing, people have asked me if I was going to the Olympics," he said. "And I always told them, 'Maybe.'" Sign two.

After that, I found our group for our last yoga session. (If I was the most seasoned skier, I was also the most miserable stretcher, hands barely dangling past my knees, groaning as I tried the Warrior Lunge, toppling when I tackled the Tree.) When we had finished our final bends, Rob called me aside and gave me his heart rate monitor to use for a few weeks until I found my own. He showed me how to strap it across my chest—it felt like some kind of talisman, as if I'd wandered into one of those scenes where the hero hands over his sword or his lariat.

The symbols were piling up too fast; I had to nasally generate some mucus to cover my emotions. But I was launched.

From the sublime to the sopping wet. I left the Berkshires that morning and drove due north, nearly to the top of Vermont, to the calendar-perfect New England village of Craftsbury Common, and then a little farther still to the Craftsbury Outdoor Center. I came because the most reliable snow in the East covers Craftsbury each winter; hence it has become a station of the cross for New England's Nordic skiers, especially those who are serious about racing. On this day, though, it felt more like Savannah. The temperatures had begun to rise steadily and the rain fell steadily. Though I didn't know it at the time, the drizzle marked the start of the most meteorologically bizarre week of the decade in the Northeast; before it ended, a mammoth ice storm had toppled whole forests across northern New York and Vermont and southern Canada, leaving millions without power. But that was down low; higher up, due to an odd temperature inversion, places like Craftsbury never saw ice. It just rained and rained and rained, with an occasional boom of January thunder to add to the biblical feel.

Craftsbury had begun the week with piles of snow, and the trails were impeccably groomed—against all odds it remained just possible to ski. And so ski I did, sweating in the dank humidity. But by week's end it was utterly comic. I went out for a long session one morning, dodging the puddles and growing bare spots, kicking on through the slush. Nine miles into a twelve-mile loop, though, I came to the Black River, which had unfrozen, swelled, and now flowed fast across a fifty-foot section of trail. It was either turn around and head nine miles back, missing lunch, or plow on through the water. Soon I was thigh-deep in the rushing snowmelt, and as branches swept by on all sides, all I could think was, what on earth am I doing here? Is this really me?

To answer this question means going back some years, back to a boyhood spent as a wimp. I'm not sure where my wimpiness came from—maybe from moving from southern California to Toronto when I was five, and hence already hopelessly behind as a hockey player, and then from Toronto to Boston when I was ten, too late to effortlessly acquire a jump shot or a home-run swing. When I ran, I ran slowly; but no gym teacher ever explained that might mean I was built for distance, not sprinting. Instead, gym became a recurring bad dream, highlighted each year by the President's Physical Fitness Test, when I got to prove to myself that I still couldn't do a pull-up. Other people despised Richard Nixon for the war in Vietnam, but I hated him because of the 600-yard run, a distance that seemed to me unimaginably long. Soon I figured out a dozen ways to stand on the sidelines or make the most token effort. If I didn't try, I couldn't humiliate myself.

By the time my father was in high school, he was tall and gangly, his hair was starting to recede, and he had a goofy happy grin. I know this from a picture that hung in the bathroom, where I saw it several times a day—the team picture from his high school baseball squad in Kirkland, Washington, now a Microsoft suburb but then a small shipbuilding town. Dad was in the back row, surrounded by lantern-jawed Swedes in their baseball flannels, young men already wearing the character of adulthood in their faces. These were the war years—no slack fleshiness. His great boyhood passion was the Seattle Rainiers, champions of the Pacific Coast League when he was nine, ten, eleven. He'd ride the ferry to Seattle and take the trolley to Sick's Stadium, to watch his hero, player-manager Jo Jo White. I once saw a flickering film of the speedy White, who used to slide into second, spikes high. "Baseball is no sissy game, and I always play for keeps," he said.

I stood the same six feet three by my senior year, with the same lanky slouch, and the same widening forehead, but if my father and I shared genes, our worlds were different. I lived in an education-obsessed suburb, where baseball was one of a thousand choices life offered a high school boy. The options ranged from dissipation to dissertation—there was a fellow in my class so mathematically advanced he was widely believed to be teaching a course at MIT. Our classrooms had the first generation of high school computers; most of my friends, even in high school, were already pre-med or pre-law or pre-something lucrative.

And yet, almost by instinct, I followed my father into the atavistic craft of journalism. He had been a newspaperman all his life—in college, and after he got out of the service. He'd worked at the *Wall Street Journal*, and at *Business Week*, and then the *Boston Globe*, where he ran the business page. By the time I reached high school, I was writing news stories and features for the local paper, but my deadline job was covering high school basketball. And what a team—state champions my senior year, beating a young Patrick Ewing in the playoffs. On Tuesday nights, Dad would drive me from the gym to the newspaper office, where he'd help me type my clichéd masterpieces, full of references to "cagers" and "hoopsters," prose that paid me twenty-five cents a column inch. He was proud of me, I knew, but I think some part of me always wondered if he'd have been prouder had I been out on the court myself.

Having convinced myself that I was a brain, not a jock, in many ways I truly ceased to care. Debate team absorbed my competitive urges—I was state champion by my senior year. I constructed my identity successfully enough, which seems to be the task of adolescence. But that identity always had a hole—the shameful sense that my body really didn't work—and that hole caused me more unhappiness than I cared to admit. I got through high school and then college without ever putting on a uniform or pinning a number on my chest, without ever challenging my assumed weeniness. In the world my dad had grown up in, I think I might have been a sissy.

Then, in my late twenties, after a stint in Manhattan writing for the *New Yorker*, I found myself living in the Adirondack

Mountains of upstate New York, the most rugged and remote corner of the East. Larger than Glacier, Grand Canyon, Yosemite, and Yellowstone combined, larger than Vermont or New Hampshire, the Adirondacks harbor only about 100,000 people. But they contain three thousand lakes, innumerable mountains, and huge unbroken forest. Growing up, I hadn't much cared for Dad's summer hiking vacations—I'd rush up trails so that I could rush back down them and return to town. But without realizing it, I'd reached an age when I was ready for the world outside. I knew I was home almost the moment I arrived in the Adirondacks—their landscape drew me in on the most visceral level. And on the most literal level too; soon I was hiking deep into the woods, paddling, snowshoeing, skiing everywhere.

My body slowly started to feel different, its inherent toughness emerging for the first time. I found, before long, that I could backpack great distances, that I loved to paddle long lakes, that nothing made me happier than all-day ski trips back of beyond. My notion of myself changed considerably, but not completely. I'd risen to some challenges (twice I traveled out west to climb Dad's iconic peak, Mount Rainier, for instance), but I still never thought of myself as an athlete. I'd never *competed*, taken on that risk to my body and my ego. In that, I was not unusual. Spectator sports have become our passion. Fewer and fewer schoolkids *play* sports each year; lots of schools have even given up on gym. And like most suburban guys my age, I'd managed to avoid the other experiences we think of as tests of manliness. There was no draft and no war when I was the right age, thank God; I never struggled to find work. Life had been—life had been easy from the start. Sometimes I felt as if I lacked something, as if the quiet strength and stability I saw in my dad had never quite taken hold in me.

Thus it was, at age thirty-seven, the age when age starts to seem like age, that I undertook this project. I decided to spend a year in real training, putting in nearly as many hours as an Olympic endurance athlete spends prepping his body. After that I would spend a winter racing. I knew I wouldn't win anything. And I knew it wasn't exciting by the standards of men's magazines: I wasn't climbing Everest on inline skates or crossing the Atlantic in an inner tube. No Raids-Gauloises for me—no eight sleepless days of kayaking Class V rivers and rappelling off thousand-foot faces. No Marathon des Sables, the week-long Saharan marathon where last year some competitors got lost in a sandstorm and spent nine days eating raw bats and sucking the water from moist towelettes. For me, just training and racing.

But that was drama enough. I wanted to see how my body would respond, and my mind, and my spirit. Partly it was pure selfishness; after a decade as an environmental writer and activist, I needed a break from failing to save the world. But mostly it was curiosity that drove me. By year's end I hoped I'd have more sense of what life lived *through the body* felt like.

Anyway, almost no one writes about sports from the point of view of the mediocre, offers insight from the middle of the pack. Thirty million Americans belong to health clubs; thirty-eight million run on treadmills, up from four million in 1987. Fifty-five million lift weights once a week, more than drop a fishhook in the water. Even if half of them are just dutifully following doctor's orders, that's a lot of athletic daydreams. And among the much smaller ranks of serious amateur athletes, I found endless frustration with the too-few hours most people had available for training; everyone wondered what it would be like to train full-time. So Walter Mitty it was.

I never had any doubt about what sport I'd pursue. Winter in the Adirondacks can last a long time, Thanksgiving to Easter in a good year. And from that moment I'd arrived in Johnsburg on a cold, snowy afternoon, it had been my favorite season. Clean, crisp, crystalline, quiet—and a pair of skis abolishes friction. Abolishes it! Perhaps because I'd spent so many years being slow, I adored the speeding glide of Nordic skis; I'd never felt graceful before, never felt elegant.

In any event, cross-country skiing meshed perfectly with my experiment, for there's no more physically demanding sport on earth. Just as swimmers use different strokes in different races, cross-country skiers compete in two separate disciplines—classic skiing, the traditional side-by-side stride that dates back to pre-historic northern Europe; and skate skiing, which uses a push-off to each side to generate momentum and which dates from the 1980s. In each case, you're using both arms and legs; you need to bull uphill and dance down; fifty-kilometer races are common-place. When exercise physiologists rank athletes by how much oxygen they can burn per minute, the biggest and best hearts and lungs in the world belong to the Norwegians, Finns, and Russians who win cross-country World Cups; they edge out even the great rowers and marathoners and Tour de France cyclists. There's nothing harder your body can do, so I figured I'd give it a try.

Exactly how hard I learned the next evening, when Rob drove over to Craftsbury from his Burlington home for dinner, and to give me my training schedule for the year to come. He decided my body could theoretically tolerate about six hundred hours of training in the next twelve months, right around the bottom of the scale for Olympic athletes. It might be too much, he stressed; I'd have to monitor myself carefully to guard against injury. He'd printed out a daily schedule, which changed through the seasons. As the year progressed, I was to work more and more on going fast. For now, though, I was to concentrate on long, slow distance, watching the readout from my heart rate monitor to make sure I didn't go too hard. "I want you spending your time in zone 1," he said, which he'd calculated by my age to be between 135 and 145 beats per minute. "You're going to be walking up hills and feeling stupid, but you need to tell yourself it's for a reason," he continued. "Before long you'll be able to ski uphill at that same heart rate."

Rob gave me one more piece of news, too. He thought I shouldn't wait until I was fully trained to begin racing; indeed, he thought I should start as soon as possible, to give my body some sense of what to expect, and my head as well. "You've got to get some experience pinning on a number," he said. In fact, he added, Craftsbury had a big race scheduled for that weekend. "Jump in the 20K," he said. "See what it feels like."

And that's how I became a Nervous Wreck. But instead of obsessing about junior high school gym class and the state of my manliness, I channeled all my worry into wax. In the brain of a committed cross-country skier, wax occupies the amount of space allotted to sex in a normal mind. Perhaps sex and money both. Wax permits you to ski uphill; if you pick the right one, the wax will grab the snow crystals as you kick the ski backward, then release them when you glide. But if wax allows cross-country skiing, it also bedevils it; different waxes work only at certain temperatures, and if you put the wrong one on the bottom of the skis, it will either clump the snow beneath your heels and act like a brake, or it will fail to grip and you will flail like a cartoon character when you try to go up even the slightest incline. On new snow, when the temperature hovers between about 20 and 27 degrees, it's easy to find the right wax. Any warmer, though, and it's very nearly impossible. That's why the pros have dozens of tubes of gooey klisters, and vials of $100-a-gram fluorocarbons; they travel to races with wax technicians and snow thermometers and electric eyes to set up elaborate speed traps and test different pairs of skis. Most purely recreational skiers, on the other hand, use skis with plastic scales on the bottom to grab the snow, but they're hopelessly slow for racing.

I had no idea what to put on for the Craftsbury race; it had finally stopped raining the morning of the race, and now the temperature was dropping fast, turning everything to ice. An hour before the start, I was still wandering around, trying to cadge advice. I asked the head of ski manufacturer Rossignol's race team, who was busy waxing skis for Olympian Marc Gilbertson, what I should use; he just glared at me as if I'd inquired about his wife's phone number and mumbled something about klister. I suppose I should have been flattered he considered me a possible threat, but I was too busy trying to get a better look at what he was spreading across the skis. It appeared to be a purplish goo, and in the small waxing hut I found another skier who lent me something vaguely similar. I smeared some on my skis, ran off to the start, and got there just as the bell sounded.

The Olympians leapt off the front of the start line, and the rest of us, maybe three hundred in all, began to sort ourselves out. The tracks were set five abreast for the first eighth of a mile, then four abreast, then three, until finally there was just a main track and a passing lane. For a couple of kilometers it was too crowded to hit any rhythm. I rode down a hill onto the back of someone's skis and knocked him over, which made me feel guilty for about a hundred yards till someone did the same to me. I was too busy dodging people to think—or really to hurt, either, though we were going hard. Then, four kilometers into the race, the course swooped down a huge hill. I snowplowed the entire way to curb my speed, and I knew as soon as I got to the bottom that the ice had scraped all the purple goo off the bottoms of my skis. Sure enough, as soon as the tracks turned uphill I started slipping backwards. Forget the graceful gliding; now there was nothing to do but herringbone, spreading my skis like wings on the snow to keep myself from sliding backwards. As I started to pant, my glasses began to fog, and soon it was like skiing through a San Francisco summer. The course looped back through the start area at 10K, where they'd mercifully set up an aid station. I drank some water and tried to wipe my glasses, but one lens immediately fell into the snow. Eventually I found it, and set out on the second lap, this time more or less by myself.

I began to calm down a little, just enough to be amazed at how fast the time seemed to pass; I'd been so focused that the forty-five minutes it took me to cover the first 10K had flown by. I didn't slow down on the second lap, either; my body was tired but not broken, and as I realized I could sort of do this, a kind of creeping exhilaration overtook me. It's true I managed to ski the wrong trail at the finish, but eventually I found where I was going—and came in under an hour and a half, a bit faster than Rob had predicted. In fact, I was right in the middle of the pack for my age. Hey, I was blooded. A new man. I probably should have quit right then and there.

# 2

The seat of the soul—sure, sure. The gauge of right and wrong, love and hate—okay. The roiling pit of the passions—why not? To an endurance athlete, though, it's mostly a pump.

But what a pump! Most of us pay no attention to our hearts. We just sit back and let them beat eternally away, the lub-dub that lulled us in our wombs, the lub-dub that won't still till we do, the eternal background noise, about as noteworthy as the hum of the refrigerator. But runners and swimmers and bikers and skiers and the like have a pumpfelt interest in their ventricles and chambers; locker room chat can suddenly swell to real pump-to-pump dialogue about stroke volume and mitochondrial density; at pump, they share a cardiac obsession.

And that's because endurance training, in essence, aims to make the pump work better. Instead of beating seventy times a minute at rest, about normal for most folks, the heart of a well-trained athlete may thump only forty-five or fifty times a minute when she's resting. Her inert body requires the same amount of blood; it's just that with each beat her heart pushes far more of it through the veins. According to Rob, who used to test the Olympic biathlon team, one of the skiers was so fit that when he woke up each morning his pulse averaged twenty-nine beats per minute. That's as impressive an achievement as buying Microsoft at six.

Almost every day of my training year I wore my heart on my sleeve—or, in warmer weather, my wrist. Within a week or two I'd mailed Rob back his heart rate monitor and acquired my own—a transmitter that wrapped around my chest, and a gaudy orange wristwatch, the Sports Instruments Circuit 7 Internal Trainer. Such monitors are barely two decades old, but they've become the basis of most endurance training. When the heart contracts, the charge passing through the cells goes from positive to negative; the transmitter picks up that charge and sends the news to your wristwatch, where the beats-per-minute indicator tells you how you're doing. Mainly it reminds you to slow down.

Before about 1980, most people trained by going hard. The immortal Czech distance runner Emil Zatopek, who ran endless solitary laps wearing his military boots, used to sprint himself into the ground at every practice. "Why should I practice running slow?" he would ask. "I already know how to run slow. I must learn to run fast." It worked for him, but for most bodies it leads to staleness, to injury. One day not long after the Craftsbury race, for instance, I found myself skiing with Phil Peck, a former national skier and onetime assistant coach of the U.S. team. "I didn't win big races till after college, till after I'd learned to train," he said. "In college I knew I could train harder than anyone else in the country, and so I did. But I went slower and slower. It took those five years to erase from my mind the misconceptions about excellence and achievement. Anyone can hammer themselves all day. To get better takes restraint."

It's so psychologically counterintuitive that most athletes, even after years of research from the physiologists, still can't grasp it. "Ninety percent of athletes train too long and hard on any given day," says Bill Corliss, who runs Sports Instruments, the monitor-maker. "I'm twenty-four years into bike racing, and I'm almost to the point where I can sometimes tell myself to back off."

Rob, whose book helped codify a new creed of low-intensity, long-duration training, could not have been more explicit. Most days, as I've said, I was not to allow my heart out of zone 1 while I was training—not to let it beat faster than 145 times a minute or slower than 135. If the trail turned uphill, it would take only a few seconds for my heart to start beating too hard, and then I would slow to a walk, feeling dorky as other skiers grunted by. But the idea was to lay a foundation—to literally change my body so that its network of capillaries would grow more dense, something that happens most easily at this gentle pace. Then, when the time came for intense training and racing, my powerful heart would have the plumbing network it needed to flush the lactic acid out of my muscles and supply fresh new blood rich with energy.

Zone 1, if you don't have a heart monitor, is the place where you can run and carry on an easy conversation. It was my address most of that winter—but I was usually alone, no one to talk to. I filled in my charts every night: two hours of skiing, three hours of skiing, marking down how my body felt, how fast my pump beat when I woke up. It required a good deal of faith in Rob, because I wanted to go fast. But it helped that once the ice storm passed the winter was cold and the snow was deep and the skiing was sublime. For several weeks it was pure delight.

And then we went to Hawaii. My wife is a writer too, and a luxe travel magazine assigned her a story that required staying at the mammoth resorts along the Kona coast of the Big Island. I went along mostly to watch over our five-year-old, Sophie, but I took my heart rate monitor with me, and instead of running the black-top through the ninety-degree lava fields, I spent the first few hours each morning in the Wellness Center or the Healthfulness Spa or whatever the gym was called in the various hotels. In truth, to call them gyms would be like calling Paris a city with some bridges and a big church. Great walls of smoked glass looked out on the ocean beaches; towels so heavy and absorbent they seemed like the pelts of exotic beasts were stacked next to bottles of distant waters; the ranks of Lifecycles and Precors and Cybexes gleamed, as attendants swiftly mopped up any hint of perspiration. I heard no grunting, just the quiet whir of pedals, the steady slap of Reebok against treadmill; and of course the never-ending voice of Bernard Shaw, patron saint of the upscale gym, delivering yet another roundup of the Lewinsky developments.

One day, halfway through a two-hour stint on the treadmill, trying to conjure up the snowy woods in my mind's eye, I glanced at the TV and saw Saddam Hussein fulminating on the screen. One of the routine crises between Iraq and the United States was flaring up, and he was preparing his country for a mighty battle. How was he preparing them? CNN showed civilians doing calisthenics in some Baghdad park, chubby middle-aged Iraqis grimacing through half-hearted sit-ups and knee bends. They must have sensed the pointlessness of it (even the most well-defined abs offer scant protection against cruise missiles), but some anachronistic genetic memory that you prepared for war by getting fit still survived in their minds. It made me wonder what other signals from remote corners of *my* psyche might be egging me on to pedal for hours going nowhere, to run fifteen miles without moving an inch.

Exercise is, after all, a bizarre discipline, even if many millions participate in it. What had seemed sublime a week before in the snow seemed insane in here. Through the windows, out past the lava-rock Jacuzzi, I could see the local surfers bobbing up and down just beyond the breakers. They seemed to be having a *great* time, completely real and very uncontrolled, exploiting the infinitely detailed and unconscious judgment that comes from thousands of hours doing something difficult. You have to be in superb shape even to paddle out through the swells, but they weren't exercising. They were not *mastering* anything, *overpowering* anything; they were collaborating with the world in all its power. It seemed the dead opposite of pounding away on the Exercycle while your heart rate monitor gently bleated.

The next morning, in two and a half hours on the recumbent bike, I read Wade Davis's classic book *One River*, an account of expeditions he and others undertook to the Amazon to track down the sources of various hallucinogenic plants. In one tribe he visited, each year on a feast day the fastest runner in the village would don women's clothes and lead all the young men on a wild chase around the borders of their territory—perhaps twenty miles long, up and down four-thousand-foot peaks, through the thick jungles. I forget what the women's clothes were about, but the run seemed to delineate in physical space their sense of collective identity.

Which was a lot more than could be said for whatever private demons I was fighting on the treadmill. I didn't even talk to the other people in the gym. Once in a locker room someone asked me if I was "a Nasdaq kind of guy or a Standard & Poor's kind of guy," but that was as close to intimacy as it got. (I couldn't bear to tell him I was an FDIC kind of guy.) People usually just stared straight ahead, lost inside their Walkmen and their dreams.

What, deep down, were those dreams? What was keeping us from the poolside, the tall drinks, the macadamia-encrusted pancakes at the breakfast buffet? Was it the desire for good health? That's the idea the fitness industry always pushes. I called up NordicTrack one day to inquire about a new ski machine, and on hold, instead of Muzak, they offered a tape loop of scary statistics and soothing solutions: "Heart disease accounts for 33 percent of all deaths in America"; "A Rand study has found that for every mile an individual walks or runs, society saves twenty-five cents in health costs."

But I already knew enough about physiology to realize that two hours on the treadmill wasn't really doing much for my health. It might be building up my capillary network, but that wasn't going to keep me alive forever. In one of the biggest studies of exercise ever done, researchers looked at 1,413 Harvard alumni: "Death rates declined steadily as energy expended on walking, stair-climbing, and sports increased from less than 500 kilocalories to 3,500 kilocalories per week, *beyond which death rates increases slightly.*" Very moderate exercise, they found, could add one to two years to a typical eighty-year lifetime. I knew this already—my father's father died at ninety-five after a life of religiously walking a few miles a day and religiously avoiding every faddish diet and fitness trend. My father was following happily in his footsteps, never having set foot on a treadmill or an Exercycle. In the words of running guru George Sheehan, "The first twenty minutes of aerobic exercise is for your body—anything beyond is for yourself." You get most of the health benefit right at the start; doing the work to turn yourself into an athlete brings at best some psychological bonus.

So why? Was I recapturing my youth or trying for a new one? As I said, I was thirty-seven, and it did seem like the very end of the possibility of youth, like the last, thinnest skim of foam lapping up to the highest point of the beach. Like 3:30 a.m. in the city, when five minutes before it was still late night, and five minutes later it will start to be early morning. If I was ever going to do such a thing, now was the moment. As Jimmy Cannon once wrote of an aging Joe Louis, struggling through a bout with Rocky Marciano, "The heart, beating inside the body like a fierce bird, blinded and caged, seemed incapable of moving the cold blood through the arteries of his rebellious body. *His 37 years were a disease that paralyzed him.*"

Still, aging didn't really obsess me. I'd watched my father grow older with good grace. He'd developed a bit of a potbelly on his lank frame, but he wore it well; it didn't seem to bother him, and though as I say he'd never to my knowledge *exercised*, his body had never let him down either. Just three years before, when he'd been sixty-five, my brother and I had hiked with him on the Wonderland Trail, a hundred miles around Mount Rainier. He'd done the same hike as a boy fifty years earlier, when they'd had to camp without fires because of the wartime blackout. If he was a bit slower now, he was still plenty fast—which he had to be to keep up with *his* brother Ernie, who was ten years older and had done the same hike *sixty* years before (carrying the same pack!).

We were already planning the next adventure—maybe something in the North Cascades. So growing older held fewer terrors for me than for some. There had to be a better reason.

The default explanation in the twentieth century is sex—if you can't figure out why you're doing something, then surely it's somehow tied up with mating. Sophie and Sue and I went out on a boat off the Kona coast one morning to watch humpback whales—a mother and a calf swimming nearby, and in the distance several males engaging in, well, athletics. Breaching, flapping their enormous tail flukes, all display designed to show the females just how robust they were. Perhaps some similar instinct explains the whole crowd of Wellness Center devotees, in our Lycra and our muscle shirts, buffing our bodies for some display. But almost everyone in the gym was past the age when reproduction should have driven their decisions, and anyway we live in an age when power, that potent aphrodisiac, flows from sources other than muscle—for proof one had only to glance up at CNN and the endless photos of our puffy president Clinton and his puffy swain.

The chemists are convinced that drugs account for all of us running the Belts to Nowhere. Endorphins to be precise, chemicals released by the body—but not until you've been exercising for about forty minutes. Not until you've gone past the "getting in shape" stage. Richard Benyo, in his book on exercise addiction, points out that many athletes will routinely aggravate injuries because they can't bring themselves to stop training, even for a day; indeed, they get jumpy and nervous if something happens at home or work that keeps them from lacing on their sneakers. "The obsessions with getting in the workout no matter what is clearly a sign of addiction . . . the athlete has gone beyond commitment and common sense, and is being driven by an irrational force," writes Benyo, who should know—he was the second man to run across Death Valley, climb Mount Whitney, and then run back. It may have been the desire for self-control or a svelte new look that got the jogger started, but Benyo says it's the tide of happy chemicals that soon drives her along.

An even better explanation of the grim dutifulness of the gym culture comes from Emily Jenkins, author of the book *Tongue First: Adventures in Physical Culture.* Jenkins taught aerobics for eight years and grew into a keen analyst of the sweating classes. "Last weekend I rode my bike along the river, dodging skaters and cyclists, joggers and speed walkers," she writes. "A few people threw Frisbees for grateful dogs or lounged on the piers, but most of us were intent on getting our heart rates into that target zone, blithely assuming that what we were doing— movement not for enjoyment, not to get anywhere, not to build anything—was entirely natural." Over time, she developed the notion that exercise for its own sake came from a longing for self-control. "One of the rhetorical standbys of the fitness industry is the phrase 'prevents aging,'" she writes. "Of course what that phrase really means is that physical effects of aging—wrinkling, sagging, bulging and hunching—can be staved off," that those bodily rebellions can be beaten back for a time. "'I was good today,' a friend will tell me. 'I ran six miles and ate really healthy.' . . . The good of fitness is about resisting temptation, working against inertia. Just like the preservation of virginity, exercising and eating right are 'good' because an outside institution (the church or the fitness industry) tells people that they are, and because they involve abstaining from something pleasurable, be it intercourse or ice cream."

Even a cursory glance around a modern gym bolsters her medievalist explanation. The ranks of weight machines are "closer to the slave-discipline contraptions of an Anne Rice porno novel than anything else I've seen in real life . . .. People open and shut their legs, pushing against metal slabs that exert pressure on their thighs . . .. They imprison themselves in the abdominal machines, looking out through a tangle of iron bars, moaning as they twist their torsos like sex-starved juvenile delinquents in a prison exploitation flick." It's a kind of punishment, a penance.

So. I strap on my heart monitor. I plug in my headphones. I tap the control panel of my treadmill, arranging for a 115-minute run at seven miles per hour on a 2 percent grade, gazing longingly out by the pool. Am I a control freak or a dope fiend? A medieval penitent or halfway to a cyborg, wanting nothing more than my soma? Isn't there something *unpathetic* to say?

Jenkins offers only one potential out for the compulsive exerciser. "The lack of games in the gym is highly significant," she writes. "These are the athletics of the fitness industry: swimming laps, running on a treadmill, pushing against machines. They are working, working out." So maybe, if I'm really training to race, I'm a mite different. "Nothing has happened in my eight years of teaching aerobics," she writes. "The tinny sounds of 80s pop were replaced by house and then by the return of 70s disco. Step aerobics were invented, but that is pretty much it. I had no wins, no losses, no last-minute scores, no sudden injuries, innovative game strategies. I had no emotional experiences whatsoever. Only a sense of control over my body, which I ultimately believe is illusory."

For endurance sports, as opposed to, say, softball or hockey, the amount of time spent training utterly dwarfs the hours spent competing. Rob's schedule for my year to come involved about six hundred hours of exercise; at most I'd spend ten to twelve hours actually racing. But I was beginning to see that those ten to twelve hours would have to emotionally justify all that endless training—that without it there really was something joyless and neutered about working out over and over and over.

Before I'd gone away, Rob had given me one extra assignment: I was to write down my goals for the end of this process, the winter racing season a year hence. I'd delayed doing it; I had no idea what I was capable of, how high I should aim. I wasn't going to win any races, I knew, but what other goals could I have? Finally I wrote: "I want to gain an intuitive sense of my body and how it works. And at least once I want to give a supreme and complete effort in a race." A *supreme* effort—how often had I mustered those in my life? Maybe once, writing my first book. That was why I was dripping a small lake of sweat beneath my Exercycle under the benevolent gaze of CNN anchor Bernie Shaw. At least, I hope it was.

# 3

Early in February, the first cross-country gold medal at the Nagano Olympics went to a Finn, Mika Myllylae, who beat the favored Norwegian, Björn Daehlie, through thirty kilometers in a raging snow. "I ski therefore I am," he told reporters after the race. His middle name, Karpasi, means "the man living in the woods and picking berries." All this I gleaned from various Web sites; on CBS, which was beaming the Nagano Games to American viewers, the Nordic races might as well have been taking place on the icy crust of some Jovian moon.

The Olympics quadrennially teases the North American fans of cross-country skiing. The world's greatest skiers have carefully peaked for the Games, ready to give the performances of a lifetime. And we *know* they are the most exciting races at the Olymics. Most of the other sports depend on gravity for their velocity, athletes rattling down the bobsled track or luge run or slalom course. For all the grace and finesse of the competitors, Isaac Newton is doing most of the actual work. The Nordic skiers must make most of the screaming turns the downhillers perform (on skinnier skis), but two-thirds of the time they're going uphill, all on their own, redlining it, trying to spend every last calorie of energy but not hit empty till the finish. Unfortunately, almost no one ever crashes spectacularly, not like the bobsledders who might sail into the hay bales, or the speed skaters always about to catch an edge, or, of course, the figure skaters who at any second could triple toe loop to tragedy, axel to oblivion. So the TV never shows it, the newspapers barely mention it, and the faithful of this small church fume and smolder.

Do they storm CBS headquarters? Boycott their advertisers? No, Nordic skiers are a mild, Saab-driving tribe. But rouse them enough and they *will* deposit sarcastic messages on your Web site. Here's a small sampling of the messages left for the network during the Games, which featured only a few moments of cross-country coverage:

> I believe that CBS (the Commercial and Bull Shit network) owes the U.S. athletes, their families, and the American people as a whole an apology for their abysmal coverage of the 1998 Winter Olympics.

> If I hear one more snippet about Tara Lipinski and her rehearsals I'm going to scream . . . Maybe if we changed the name to cross-country ice-dancing it would get some coverage.

> I am so incensed! In the middle of my very satisfying evening of watching CBS Olympic coverage of Tara practicing her maneuvers and some very tastefully done credit card and automobile

commercials, I was confronted with well over a minute of the 30 kilometer men's classic race. The time used for this coverage, easily a full minute, could have been much better spent on more figure skating practice.

And it wasn't just TV that looked the other way. On February 16, the day after the immortal Daehlie became the first person to win six winter gold medals, the *New York Times* offered him six paragraphs. He was a minor footnote to the day's big question: Should a Canadian snowboarder keep his gold even though he tested positive for marijuana?

It's all especially frustrating to Nordic skiers because their small church—almost reduced to a cult, like rowing—looked for a time as if it might be the next great American sport. Its moment of glory came in the winters of the 1970s, when the new wave of joggers turned to cross-country skiing for cold-weather workouts. John Caldwell, who'd been coaching at a prep school in southern Vermont, managed to sell half a million copies of his guide to the sport. Len Johnson, a Swede transplanted to New Hampshire, recalls showing up at the annual Washington's Birthday race at Jackson in 1975. Theretofore a small gathering of the faithful, all of a sudden it had attracted a thousand skiers crowding the start line.

Whether chicken or egg, that boom also produced a wave of elite skiers able to race with the Russians and the Scandinavians. Caldwell coached most of them at the Putney Ski Club, including his son Tim and Bill Koch, America's single Nordic star, who actually managed to win a silver medal at the 1976 Winter Olympics in Innsbruck. I went to Putney to talk to Caldwell senior one summer day and found him brewing beer in his kitchen, occasionally stalking off down the hill to stoke the fire in his sauna. At seventy-eight, he still gave some signs of the crustiness he once brought to coaching. "When it started to hurt, I would just yell at them, scream at them," he said. "I'd have local kids, their parents were farmers maybe, and they were just gritty. I'd have everyone line up and I'd say, 'You're going to run this hill for me.' You're dying, but the guy next to you is gritting it out. What are you going to do? Stop? And then they'd finish and I'd say, 'Find someone your same weight, and let's see how fast you get up the hill with someone on your back.'"

Whatever he and the coaches, like Marty Hall and Mike Gallagher, who followed him, were doing with those small groups of skiers, it worked—through the mid-1980s, the Americans skied as fast as anyone else in the world. "We had four or five finishing in the top twenty at all the races," recalls Phil Peck, the assistant coach at the end of that stretch. "Kochie won the World Cup one year, and all the rest of them thought they could too. It was terribly exciting just to go to the races."

And then, as quickly as they had begun, both the boom in skiing and the burst of racing success began to wind down. When Koch, Caldwell, and the rest retired, no one was ready to follow them. John Caldwell feuded with the sport's governing body; Peck ended up teaching Russian history and coaching the skiers at Holderness, another New England prep school. One of the few remnants of the period are the "Bill Koch leagues," the Little Leagues of Nordic skiing; nationwide a few thousand youngsters compete, but Peck says even that has been a mixed blessing. "We had their big New England festival here at Holderness a few years ago, and it was terrible—all those parents out there yelling at their kids. You don't need to give them split times when they're ten years old;

you need to be showing them fun. The top kids from those leagues rarely go on to compete at college—they're burned out."

Whatever the reason, American skiers haven't come close in recent years; to finish in the top twenty-five of an international race has become a moral victory. And the number of just plain skiers has dwindled too. If you want to find a gloomy group of salesmen, look no further than those charged with selling Nordic skis to Americans. Steve Quinaug, a Norwegian who once made the junior national team as a ski jumper, now lives in New Hampshire, where he oversees North America for Alpina, a top boot maker. I went by his office one day in the middle of winter and found him almost cowering behind his desk. "It hasn't snowed all winter in the Midwest, and my sales reps are afraid to call their dealers for fear they'll want to ship the product back." In Burlington, Vermont, John Schweizer tries to market the impressive Peltonen skis, which he imports from Finland. But "the base of our pyramid has just collapsed," he says. "It's weird, too, because the demographics are perfect. There's the aging baby boom population who should be retiring from downhill, there's no better fitness sport on earth, you don't have to wreck your joints." Peter Hiller, an Austrian who leads Fischer's Nordic division, says much the same thing is happening worldwide, despite the pockets of rabid skiers in northern Europe. "When I started ten years ago, the world market was 2.1 million pairs; now it's down to just over a million."

Everyone has a theory for the dip. New sports have emerged—mountain bikes and snowboards hadn't been invented when Koch won his silver medal, and snowshoes have been transformed from utilitarian backcountry transit into expensive toys that appear on Mountain Dew commercials. Maybe cross-country skiing seems too hard to people. "We want to go for the thirty-five to sixty demographics," says Peltonen's Schweizer. "We want to make it the low-impact outdoor social exercise." Or maybe it seems too easy. "The little old lady who sees an ad on TV is not going to come skiing," says Fischer's Ron Norton. "We have to attract the cross-trainers. We need the athletic lifestyle people, the guy who's riding his bike on rollers in the garage all winter."

Everyone agreed on one thing, however—winter, and especially the recent lack of it, makes Nordic skiing a tenuous enterprise. I've obsessed about global warming for more than a decade; my books on the topic have been translated into twenty-two languages; I've written hundreds of articles, given hundreds of speeches. But I've never found an audience as receptive as ski salesmen. "We feel it already," says Hiller, the dour Austrian who runs Fischer's cross-country division. "The average altitude where we have a steady snow covering is going up the last ten years." Indeed it is; spring comes a week earlier to the Northern Hemisphere on average than it did just two decades ago—spring comes a week earlier than when Bill Koch won his medals. Torny Mogren, one of the great Swedish ski champions of the 1980s, told a Stockholm paper not long ago that he wanted his son to play tennis or golf "because the snow conditions are so different from when I was a kid." While I was slogging through the rain at Craftsbury, NASA declared 1997 the warmest year on record.

So, a cult, and a cult that may be doomed to ever-muddier winters, ever-earlier springs. Cross-country skiers may be the Shakers of sport, and like the Shakers in their day subject to every kind of ridicule. *Skiing* magazine, the alpine bible, recently offered an appraisal of the sport under the headline "Life Is an Endless

Catwalk and Other Inanities of Cross Country Skiing." Among
other things, it described Nordic skiers as "bone thin, with sunken
eyes, elbows that could pick locks, and doleful demeanors." Once
again, the Nordic Web sites thrummed with anger—"a stab in the
back," said one ski area manager, while another called for a class-
action lawsuit in defense of cross-country skiing, demonstrating
the same robust sense of humor as, say, Ted Kaczynski.

Still, the Shakers went out singing, and in certain ways Nordic skiing, too, is at its peak of glory. The sport has never had a
champion to match Daehlie, the Norwegian wunderkind recently
voted "Nordic athlete of the *millennium*." I've watched the videos
of his greatest races a hundred times, and his instructional tape
too, which is filled with Puritan advice. "Do not think you can
spend the summer riding the mountain bike and expect to win
races," he says sternly, prescribing instead an austere regime of
"hill bounding" and "sideways hill bounding." By some accounts,
Daehlie trains as much as a thousand hours a year—and he's done
it for fifteen seasons. At the end of every race he flings himself
across the line, spent, and few of his competitors accuse him of
showmanship. Now, finally, his greatest moment comes at the
Nagano Games. On the last afternoon of the Olympics, in the
sport's premier event, the fifty-kilometer classic race, Daehlie col-
lapses at the finish. He's won by eight seconds, his body so
wracked that handlers have to pack him in ice for an hour to cool
him down. His eighth gold medal moves him ahead of anyone else
in Winter Olympics history.

And on TV? The figure skating gold medals had been awarded
the night before, so this night CBS decided to show an exciting
*exhibition* performance by the skaters.

• • •

While the gods like Daehlie are contesting World Cup races across northern Europe each weekend, the lay adherents of this sect gather instead for a series of great marathons spread across the hemisphere. The Birkebeiner, held early each spring in Lilleham-mer, is the most famous of all, drawing nearly ten thousand Nor-wegians for a fifty-eight-kilometer trek across the mountains; the American Birkebeiner, in Hayward, Wisconsin, is this continent's biggest race. Somewhat smaller, but closer to my home, Ottawa hosts the Keskinada festival each February. Since it was a few hours away, I decided to go double my total racing experience. As it turned out, I had a good deal to learn.

Our hotel in Ottawa looked out over the Rideau Canal, crowded with thousands of skaters. I'd been checking in over the phone with Rob every few days, and at his urging I took it easy the day before the race—half an hour on the treadmill to take the driving rust out of my legs, and then off to a café to eat noodles. I felt more on top of things here in Ottawa than I had in Crafts-bury because my friend Jack Burke, an Adirondack neighbor and longtime racer, had offered to wax my skis. Actually, he'd volun-teered his son, Tim, and Tim's friend Lowell Bailey. They are hot junior skiers—biathletes, actually, adherents of a splinter sect whose members ski and then stop to shoot at targets. Compared to *their* heroes, Björn Daehlie is as overexposed as Princess Di. But they know how to wax—they are always coming back from the Jura or the Apennines with mysterious vials of powder, secret tubes of paste. So what could go wrong? I watched the double-lugers from Nagano on TV (a Newtonian sport if there ever was one) and then slept soundly.

By the time I woke at five-thirty, a bitter cold front had pushed through—the temperature had dropped way below zero. Still, I knew I'd soon be sweating, so I put on one thin pair of Polypro long johns and my new Lycra racing suit, and headed out the door. Tim and Lowell met me in the parking lot near the start line and fired up their propane torch to melt in a layer of sticky klister for grip on the icy snow, then rubbed in some glide wax impregnated with expensive fluorine to make the skis glide easily. I tested them out; they were silky fast, and I couldn't wait to start.

Which was the moment Jack chose to tell a funny story about a race he'd been at years before when one of his fellow racers, on a windy bitter day just like this, had gone off without his windbriefs, only to have his penis freeze right up. *His penis froze right up!* Ha ha ha!

Hearing no laughter from me, Jack looked over. "Uh oh," he said.

"What's a windbrief?" I asked.

It turns out that on cold days, since Lycra does little to cut the wind, ski racers wear fleece-lined jockstraps, or underwear with a plastic panel on the fly. As it also turns out, I wasn't the first one to make this error. Months later, reading John Morton's biathlon novel, *Medal of Honor*, I came across a classic description of "hooter freeze" ("athletes were moaning in pain, rocking back and forth on the cots"). But even if I'd known it, that would have come as very cold comfort. Already I could feel things shriveling.

Before I could worry any more, the horn sounded for the start, and my wave of several hundred skiers headed out through a field and then up a series of hills. My wax worked, the trail was fast, but I was lost in a series of conjectures about my reproductive organs. Normally I don't spend too much of the day thinking about my member, but now I could think of little else; on the downhills, when the wind would whistle even faster, I'd pull my fanny pack around in front and crouch behind it like a shield, sacrificing a second or two of speed for a degree or two of windchill factor. I remember stopping for a quick shot of hot lemonade halfway through the 20K course, and I remember, as seemed to be my habit, taking a wrong turn near the end. I got back on track, flew across the finish, and headed straight for the men's room, where I spent the next half hour whimpering. If the s&m community has not yet discovered the pastime, I am thinking of organizing package tours to the northland. All in all, a memorable day.

Tim and Lowell were still wandering around the parking lot when I finally warmed up enough to leave. "Hey, nice race," said Tim. "You weren't the last by any means." And I retained my dick! Reason enough to declare it a victory. Suitably bundled, Sue and Sophie and I spent the afternoon skating on Ottawa's magic canals and the evening consuming vast quantities of onion rings.

That night on TV, Canadian Skater Elvis Stojko managed a silver-medal finish, but the second he was done his stage grin morphed into a grimace. It turned out he'd pulled his groin months before and had been carefully hiding his distress throughout the competition. He'd calibrated perfectly, saving just enough energy to get through his performance, but he was so spent he couldn't even skate out to get his medal. I decided that the best thing about cross-country skiing was that you could grimace *during* the race and no one minded.

# 4

Sometimes you find yourself in places where you simply don't belong. I was already lined up at the starting gate with the other thirty-five- to thirty-nine-year-olds when I noticed that not only were they whippet-thin and bulldog-strong, but also that almost none of them spoke English. They chattered away in—well, I could make out German, and Italian, and I guessed at Swedish and Norwegian. "Dasvydonya," someone said as I let him by, and sure enough he was wearing an old CCCP warmup. I wanted suddenly to leave, but there was only one way out of that start area, and that was down the parallel tracks directly in front of me.

Under normal circumstances, Rob would never have let me go to the World Master Championships that first winter of my training. But by coincidence, the annual event wasn't being held in Zermatt or Oslo or Lahti; it was making an extremely occasional visit to the States, and indeed to my Adirondacks—to the course at Lake Placid's Mount Van Hoevenberg that had hosted the 1980 Olympics. All the local skiers had talked of little else since the first snows fell in November; and perhaps we were a little lulled by the idea that these were "masters" skiers—it sounded almost gentle.

Masters athletics is relatively new, but booming. For cross-country skiers, masters competitions begin at thirty, which may be a bit early—the best skiers in the world peak at just about that age, and a thirty-nine-year-old Finn had just won a medal in the Olympic relay and announced he wasn't planning to retire. From the looks of those who were skiing by me as I practiced the day before the Lake Placid race, some of these people should have been in Nagano too. Even the eighty- and ninety-year-olds looked fast in their Lycra racing suits.

No one really knows when athletes start getting old; for every Joe Louis who wore his thirty-seven years like a coat of rust, there's a Nolan Ryan coming into his own at forty. The first modern endurance athletes, the early Olympic champions, were mostly American college students—the gospel of the day, according to Allan Lawrence and Mark Scheid in their book *Running and Racing After 35*, was that twenty-one was the last really good year for racing. Now the common wisdom is that endurance athletes peak between twenty-seven and thirty—but Carlos Lopes won the Olympic Marathon in 1984 at the age of thirty-six, beating the favorites Rob de Castella (twenty-nine) and Alberto Salazar (twenty-six). Priscilla Welch won the women's New York City Marathon at the age of forty-three: "You know what a vintage car is like," she said later. "You learn to flick open the hood a bit more and tickle it and replace parts." There's physiological reason to expect you'd lose a step or two—a sedentary fifty-year-old has only 80 percent of the cardiovascular efficiency he had at thirty, his lung capacity has dropped by a quarter, and his nerve impulses fire 5 percent less quickly. As Samuel Johnson once remarked, "He who competes against time has an adversary who does not suffer casualty." But who knows how much of that loss can be reversed by keeping in competition shape? "We have no real idea of how much you lose," said New York masters swim coach Conrad Johnson. "Almost no one's ever trained continuously from thirty to fifty."

One of the explorers on this frontier is John Brodhead, who runs the Craftsbury ski area where I'd spent that soggy week at the start of my year. He comes from a classic ski background—his father was a headmaster at a New Hampshire prep school that boasted, among other things, its own ski-jumping hill. He spent the winters downhilling and the summers cutting brush for new trails with his hatchet; to earn a Boy Scout merit badge he taught himself to cross-country ski, and then put his knowledge to use in high school, where ski meets went like this: "In the morning you'd go and do the slalom, and then you'd sidestep up the hills to pack the downhill trails. Right after lunch they did the jumping, and then you'd take off your stretch pants and put on your knicker suit for the cross country." Middlebury College was lousy with alpine skiers when Broadhead arrived, but there was room on the Nordic roster; specializing, he managed to place in the top five or ten consistently at all the biggest races.

And there the story probably should have ended—he wasn't quite fast enough to make the national team or the Olympics. But he never stopped skiing—not at grad school in western Massachusetts, not as a young Ph.D. biology teacher at Mount Holyoke. Having located a like-minded bride, he spent his honeymoon at the World Masters in Oslo—"I thought I'd died and gone to heaven. The thousands of kilometers of trails, the way they lived, the way they kept themselves fit." Eventually he moved to northern Vermont and took charge of the Craftsbury program, which left him with even more time to ski. "I've been in racing shape for thirty-six or thirty-seven years without missing a season," he said. "It's a source of pride to me, something I like to think about. I think I have one of the lowest numbers of a competition license in the U.S. Ski Association—my high school coach made me apply when I was thirteen or fourteen." He skis—or roller-skis—one long slow workout every week, three hours at a minimum, and at least one session of hard intervals and another five or ten kilometers at racing pace. "If there wasn't racing, I wouldn't train as hard, I don't think. But I really feel fulfilled if I have a good hard interval workout—it's a mind-over-matter thing. Sometimes this year I've gone out and really pushed myself, and I almost actually enjoyed the feeling even while I was doing it. I could really get beyond the pain, the exertion."

So that morning in Lake Placid, when I saw John Brodhead waxing his skis, carefully and doggedly, without a second to spare for small talk, I began to sense just how far in over my head I actually was. We were going thirty kilometers, half again as far as I'd ever raced before, and from the moment the gun sounded I was hopelessly behind. Cross-country races begin with a hundred yards of double-poling; instead of moving your feet you just push with your arms, bobbing up and down like a railway inspector powering a track car. When the hundred yards was past, all I could see in front of me was a parade of spandex-encased Scandinavian backside. I was wearing my fleecy new jock. My wax was speedy. (A perfectionist neighbor, John

Underwood, was working for one of the wax companies, and he'd spent the previous day running skis through electric eyes. "This stuff is almost 20/100ths of a second faster over thirty meters," he'd assured me. "Think what that means over thirty kilometers.") The only things I lacked were strength, stamina, skill, and will. By the time we'd gone one kilometer, the end of the train of skiers was disappearing away in the distance. My wife, who was watching, told me later there were actually two skiers from my wave trailing me, but I thought I was dead last. And I knew I was too slow to catch those in front of me; I was pretty sure I'd bury myself if I tried. A good decision, for as it turned out the competition was even tougher than I'd imagined; the guy who eventually won my age group, the guy leading that express train out in front of me, had taken an Olympic bronze just a couple of years before.

So I skied the first of two 15-kilometer loops pretty much by myself, filling my brain with exactly the sort of negative talk— "what a loser"—that Rob kept warning me against. Forget your boyhood clumsiness, he'd tell me. "It's like you have a wise friend, but at a party one night you see him really going for it, drinking it up. That's not when you're going to ask him for heavy advice. That's sort of like all of us in our youths—don't listen too carefully to that person." But it was hard not to, especially as the faster skiers in the next wave—the forty- to forty-five-year-olds— made up my five-minute head start and began to roar by. I'd try to stick with them for a few seconds and then fall back. As I passed through the stadium at the halfway point, Rob was there to hand me water and tell me I was looking good, which was such an outrageous fib I loved him for making it. I wasn't at all sure I wanted to even *do* lap 2, but my daughter was watching.

And then something happened. Up ahead I caught sight of another member of my wave, #2009, who had gone out fast and evidently slowed down a little. I'd seen him as we went up hills; by the time I reached the top he'd have vanished, but on the next hill he'd be a bit closer. All of a sudden it didn't matter that the best fifty-five-year-olds were grunting past, demanding in Kazakh or Moldovan that I clear the way. All of a sudden I was racing. Eventually 2009 pulled over at the top of a hill, maybe eight kilometers from the finish, where his girlfriend was waiting with a water bottle. I went right past, high as a kite—maybe I wouldn't be last after all.

A few minutes later, though, I heard something flopping and looked down to see that the ankle strap on my ski boot was loose. I tried to stop and fix it, but before I could get it Velcro-ed back together, old 2009 ripped by me again, so I just stood up and chased. Though my foot was threatening to slip out of the boot, I stayed with him stride for stride—he'd get a couple of feet ahead, then I'd catch him, back and forth. Mouse and mouse.

Finally, at the top of a small rise about three kilometers from the finish, he just pulled over to the side of the trail and let me go. But by this point I was watching the kilometer markers with almost desperate eagerness; I know I can do 3K more, I kept telling myself. That's barely from my house to the lake and back. The 2K sign went by, and the 1K, and then with about three-quarters of a kilometer to go I suddenly felt as if all the blood in my body had been drained away. My legs wanted badly not to go, I was stumbling over my poles, my ears were roaring. I somehow topped a small rise, and there was calm Rob skiing alongside me, telling me I'd gone faster the second lap than the first, telling me I looked good.

In point of fact, I looked *ugly*—an icy slick of splittle clung to my chin. Something about all-out exertion in freezing weather makes mucous control difficult—Nordic racers often cross the line looking like four-year-olds with nasty colds. (Only a few weeks earlier, Marc Gilbertson had won a race to make the Olympic team and then spent his fifteen minutes of relative fame giving interviews with something ropy hanging from his nostrils. "They called me Boogerman," he said.) But in some deeper sense, I knew Rob was right. I'd finished twenty-seven minutes behind the winner, but I was twenty-seven seconds ahead of 2009, and as it turned out a couple of others from my wave really *were* behind me too. I was twenty-ninth in a field of thirty-three, but I was first in my little contest, and I began to sense a few of the attractions of racing. Partly it was the simple test, of course—the surge of good feeling that comes with fighting through some challenge. I hadn't dogged it after all; I'd chased old 2009 down twice, and I'd finally gone right through him.

Even stronger, though, was the feeling of total clarity that had come over me in that small drama. For once in my life I was absolutely present, right there the whole time. For one hour, 56 minutes, 37 and $\frac{3}{10}$ths seconds, almost every thought that flashed in my brain concerned that race, that moment. As I drove myself harder, my field of thought shrunk down to a narrow focused tunnel. I was monitoring my body—legs, lungs, arms—trying to make sure I stayed close to the edge, going as fast as I could without draining my tanks too quickly. I counted the kilometer markers, I watched the tracks for every rise and corner that might give me some advantage, and that was that. None of the endless internal CNN. The stopless chatter that usually fills my brainpan, broadcasting my moods, fantasies, plans, regrets, and glories,

ceased, and only the moment existed. It wasn't entirely unfamil-
iar; sometimes when I'm writing that sense of flow kicks in, and
sometimes in sex. Occasionally I've taken solo backpacking trips
long enough that my mind has run short of junk food and quieted
down. But the almost-desperate clarity of this race attracted me
enormously. I stood up and cheered at the awards ceremony that
night when John Brodhead collected his silver medal, but the clear
fast that I was never going to win any hardware suddenly mattered very little. I'd like another fix of that total absorption,
please.


The next chance—the last chance for the winter—came in late
March on the Tug Hill Plateau. Tug Hill may be the strangest bit
of geography in the lower 48, a tiny world apart, though you'd
never guess it during the summer. It rises just east of Lake Ontario,
perfectly poised to catch the "lake effect" snow that falls whenever weather from the Canadian plains moves across Ontario's
open waters. It's nothing for two or three feet of snow to fall in a
single day, even when it's bright and sunny at my house sixty
miles away; on the Tug Hill Plateau, the fat flakes *hurry* out of
the sky, as if to make room for all that must follow. So much
snow falls that the drifts linger on into the spring. When the other
ski touring centers are starting to grease up the fleet of rental
bikes for the summer season, Hans Giuliani is still plowing the
parking lot and grooming the trails at Salmon Hills, the resort he
runs in the heart of the Tug Hill. "Once last year we got seven
feet of snow in two days," he said. "I couldn't get out of the
groomer for days. If I had stopped grooming, I'd never have been
able to find the track again."

When I arrived for the season's last race, in mid-March, snow was cascading down as usual, and the banks were shoveled high around the tentlike yurts that provide the main accommodation. I settled in the bunkhouse, where a kind of philosopher-king named John Spas was cooking dinner and holding forth. A sporting goods salesman from Syracuse sixty miles to the south, Spas got into skiing so that he could stay in shape for his real love, ultramarathon bicycling. In particular, he gears his year to the Boston-Montreal-Boston race, 1,200 kilometers with 30,000 feet of climbing through the Green Mountains. "My legs are pretty serious legs," he said. "I have friends who ride along at twenty-one and a half miles per hour, laughing and giggling, and I can't do that. But if you want someone to ride between seventeen and nineteen miles per hour for three days, I'm your man."

And your man, too, if you want advice. Some of it was practical. ("In the morning be sure to evacuate your colon. That's when you're really ready to go. Of course, during the Boston-Montreal I don't defecate at all.") Most of his words were spiritual, though. "It's all a matter of preparation—opportunity—success," he insisted. And "you can constantly improve; it has far more to do with your mental hygiene than your training." And "when you're going up that hardest hill, be thinking of the smell of your grandmother's cologne, or being intimate with some woman you've not been intimate with." And, most memorably, this piece of advice: "At every endurance event, there comes a time when you'll say, 'What the fuck am I doing here?' And you'll say, 'This is what I do.'"

The next morning's race looped around a fifteen-kilometer course; I'd planned to do one or maybe two of the laps, but with Spas's aphorisms pumping me up, the thought of going all forty-five kilometers began to creep into my mind. It was farther than I'd ever raced; at about thirty miles, it was probably farther than I'd ever skied. And this would be my first skating race, where the parallel kick-and-glide of "classic" cross-country skiing is replaced by the side-to-side push-off motion of an ice skater. Not only that, but all the new snow was soft and deep, making the going harder. For the first lap, which took about an hour, I concentrated on a slow, steady pace; the second time around I chased a couple of college boys for a little while, until they'd outdistanced me.

My legs still felt reasonable, though, so I decided to go the whole distance, and as I began the last lap I found myself in a pack of five skiers, including another fellow who'd spent the night on the bunk next to mine. He was just a little arrogant; maybe his sunglasses were just a bit too cool—suddenly there was a bit of sporting interest. We skated together down a series of hills and out onto a frozen lake, where we skied perhaps a kilometer with the wind at our backs and then turned a sharp corner and headed back into the stiffening breeze. Mr. Shades poured it on, saying a perhaps well-intentioned "good luck" to me as he sprinted away. I decided to take it the wrong way and follow him; by the time we made it back to the woods there were only the two of us left from our pack of five. The last five kilometers tended uphill, and we were both pretty bushed, but with a kilometer left to go I managed to power past him on a steep ascent and then stay just ahead. The race ended with a curving downhill turn, and my legs were gone. I thought I might fall, but I didn't, and crossed the line still in the lead.

I was perhaps half an hour back of the winner—the fastest guys had already showered and dressed—and yet once more I felt like, well, an athlete. I'd been in some other zone on the last lap;

I'd come up against John Spas's question, and at least for an hour been able to say, "This is what I do."

Endurance sports really *are* different. A sprint finishes before you can think about it, but a long race involves altogether too many opportunities to consider. Rich Kenah, the American 800-meter champion, told me once that "the thought process of a 400-meter runner is, I want to get around the track as fast as I can. By the 800 meters, it's, I want to get around the track as fast as I can without slowing down in the middle. The longer you go, the more time there is to think about quitting partway through." That's why the battle for 253rd place in a marathon can be just as gripping as the battle for first.

I'm not talking about those competitors determined to simply finish the race. They have a dignity and a psychology all their own, as more and more Americans are discovering. The fastest-growing ranks in every marathon, are the so-called penguins, a name bestowed by *Runner's World* columnist John Bingham, whose T-shirt says, "I Know, I'm Slow, Get Over It." Plenty of those penguins never imagined they could do such a thing—finishing, even at a trot designed to keep their pain to a minimum, may change their lives in a more profound way than anything I'm doing.

The people who interest me even more, though, are the *racers*, the people who, however slow, are trying to go as fast as they can and not worry about keeping the pain at bay. What masters runner would race the hundred-meter dash year after year if he always came in near last? All he'd prove is that he was slow. But in a race that lasts long enough for will to become as important as physiology or training, you can win or lose as easily in the middle of the pack as at the front. You can win or lose a dozen times; if you wimp out on the first lap, you can step up on the third. There are as many dreams, triumphs, and desolations among the mediocre endurance athletes as among the stars. It's the closest thing sports offers to a democracy.

# 5

The healthiest-looking people I met that winter weren't athletes at all. Or maybe in a way they were. I left the frozen Northeast for a few days and flew to California—to another ashram, this one in Marin, where an elderly Indian named Eknath Easwaran led a small collective of serious meditators. By serious, I mean that some of them sat cross-legged four hours a day, and many had been doing it for more than thirty years, ever since the time in the mid-1960s when Easwaran arrived in Berkeley from India to teach the first college course on meditation. On assignment from a magazine, I'd come to interview him about Gandhi—Easwaran had met him as a young man, and the encounter had helped change his life. But I'd also read Easwaran's books over the years and tried sporadically to follow his commonsense plan for meditation.

If nature had left me with slow-twitch muscles, nurture had given me a fast-twitch mind; for me, meditation meant trying desperately to keep my mind on the passage I'd memorized while a train of magnetic thoughts passed by, each one trying to lure me into thinking it. Usually I did; my half-hour morning sittings were so disappointing I never lasted more than a few months at a stretch. (That's probably why the clarity of racing attracted me so much—for an hour I was simply *there* and nowhere else.) But I knew from the calmness of Easwaran's prose that he was the real item. The relaxed, happy faces of his followers said the same thing. They weren't zealots—they seemed, though, nearly to burst with good health, mental and physical and most of all emotional. And they'd done it in a way that was increasingly familiar to me: through untiring discipline. Not just through meditation: Easwaran's program also involves repeating a mantram, slowing down, making sure to do only one thing at a time, systematically putting the wishes of others first, and training the senses with simple food. "If you see a car with a bumper sticker that says 'Easy Does It'—that's not my car," said Easwaran. His discipline is, in short, a way of life, designed to produce a better human being—a Gandhian program.

When I told Easwaran about my endless skiing, he recalled watching the Los Angeles Olympics a few years earlier. "I was watching the swimming and I was astounded how young many of the great athletes were," he said. "And yet, while they may have had some natural gifts, I am inclined to think it is essentially their dedication under a very demanding and loving teacher that is responsible for their success. Their style was so beautiful—with the minimum effort they got the maximum results."

Having recently acquired a guru of my own, I was inclined to agree. And to agree as well that the achievements even of Olympians paled next to the achievements of people who had mastered the art of daily life. "In the modern world, it's very difficult to come across a coach who will show you how to increase your security, how to return good will for ill will, how to turn your back on your own satisfaction to contribute to the well-being of your neighbor and your world," said Easwaran. As a young man he'd watched Gandhi, that insubstantial vegetarian fakir, walk hundreds of miles under the blazing sun to protest one injustice or another, seen him fast nearly to the death again and again to stop some slaughter, seen him endure jail cheerfully. His followers here in Marin were spiritual athletes, unassuming but powerful, exploring how to be a man in the best sense of the word, or a woman. They were going after something harder and higher than I was.

So far, in fact, this year of training desperately had been an exercise in solipsism. As Rich Kenah, the 800-meter champion, said to me one day, "To be a truly dedicated endurance athlete is to be selfish. To live within your own inner circle, without much room for anyone but yourself. My family, my friends, my job have gotten the short end of the stick. I have to protect my time, my resources, my energy." His honesty had a familiar ring. For a decade I'd worked pretty faithfully on environmental causes; now I was turning down every request for help. I tried to make sure I didn't neglect my family, but there were plenty of Saturday mornings I could have horsed around with Sophie instead of heading off for another run. My schedule ruled the day—I didn't relax until I'd ticked off the minutes on my chart, and as soon as I had, I began thinking about the day to come.

All I could tell myself was, just maybe, that I was learning some new level of concentration and discipline that would make me a—well, better person too. That all this training was functioning as a kind of meditation, that it might turn me into someone who didn't snap so often at my child, might transform me into a truer kind of spouse. That my current selfishness might someday yield a man who could more reliably put himself second. That it might, in other words, make me more like my dad, who through some fortune or some effort had emerged by the time I knew him as a thoroughly graceful human being. In all the years of my growing up, I'd never heard him get angry at Mom (or she at him). He'd dealt with my rebellions mildly, calmly—not, at least in my recollection, with the grit-toothed scowl that Sophie's five-year-old craziness could produce in me. In fact, the maddest I ever remember him getting was one day when I said something mean to Mom. And even then it was more bewilderment than sadness. "Don't you know you have the greatest mother in the world?" he'd asked. Why the hell was I so peevish some days? Would bigger lungs make me a bigger man?

Quite likely it was folly to even think so. Coaches and ex-football players are forever talking about sports as a lesson for life, but then they're also claiming that Jesus takes a deep interest in the trajectory of their field goal attempts. Much saner, probably, to see sport as simply one more hobby, like building fantastically detailed model railroad layouts in your garage with real steam puffing from the tiny locomotive as it endlessly circles the track. Still, I was far from the first to wonder if there might be some connection between cardiovascular and character development. In his book *Running Wild*, John Annerino tells tales of his own quest for meaning through desert running—47,240 miles of it between 1976 and 1997. But even more he describes those who had come before: the Hohokam people, say, who a thousand years ago would make 200-mile ritual journeys to the Pacific to gather seashells, and their descendants who ran the same course to gather salt. As one tribal elder wrote:

> Many people
> just run for miles and
> never get any power
> from the ocean.
> I suppose there are but very few
> who make their luck and become somebody
> or know something.

It's that elusive *knowing something* that draws one on; surely all this work must teach *some* eternal truth.


In Tibet, the *lung gompas*, or "running lamas," mastered a kind of mystical marathoning; in order to run several hundred miles on pilgrimages across the 12,000-foot-high plateau, they would train by staying virtually motionless in complete darkness for three years and three months. Alexandra David-Neels writes, "It must be understood that the *lung gom* method does not aim at training the disciple by strengthening his muscles, but by developing psychic states that make those extra-ordinary marches possible." If only. By contrast, as the snow started to melt and friction began to reassert itself, I was pretty much in perpetual motion.

On the last few skis of the year, the stronger sun was melting out the twigs and stones along the track—glide began to turn to lurch. I'd cross streams, and the snowbridge would crumble into the water behind me. When my brother and I were growing up, our parents read us the Narnia series over and over, and this quick spring reminded me of that fine moment in *The Lion, the Witch, and the Wardrobe* when the good lion Aslan begins to melt the White Witch's eternal winter: "Every moment the patches of green grew bigger and the patches of snow grew smaller. Every moment more and more of the trees shook off their robes of snow. Soon, wherever you looked, instead of white shapes you saw the dark green of firs or the black prickly branches of bare oaks and beeches and elms."

Truth be told, for a few weeks spring felt just fine to me. Each year when it first warms, I can feel my shoulders unhunching. It's only then that I realize how folded in on myself I've gotten during the coldest stretches of winter. There was something novel about running deep into the woods or even along the shoulder of the road; I'd never been in the kind of shape before that allowed me to run for a couple of hours and not think much of it. As the spring wore on, though, those runs grew longer and longer. Under Rob's plan, spring and summer called for the most mileage. A typical week, by no means the longest, looked something like this:

Sunday: 205 minutes (that's about 3-½ hours) of what Rob called "overdistance," running just fast enough to keep my heart rate between 135 and 145 beats per minute, with a 30-second burst of pure speed every 20 minutes or so just so my muscles didn't forget how to fire more quickly.

Monday: 61 minutes of "endurance" training, moving fast enough that my heart beat about 150 times a minute. Then 80 minutes of strength training—in my case, climbing aboard one of Rob's inventions, the Vasa Trainer, a sliding-seat contraption that mimics cross-country's poling motions. And at night, half an hour of trying to stretch my rigid old body into the Kneeling

Crescent Moon and the Butterfly, and the Camel with Twist.

Tuesday: 102 minutes of overdistance.

Wednesday: 164 minutes of overdistance, and another 80 minutes on the Vasa Trainer, more stretching.

Thursday: 41 minutes of overdistance, and 61 minutes of "uphill intervals," sprinting up slopes at my aerobic threshold of 165 beats per minute.

Friday: 82 minutes of overdistance, more time on the Vasa Trainer, another session of attempted yoga.

Saturday: blessed rest.

Most of the time I followed my program with blind faith, like an old-time penitent told to say twenty Our Fathers. If Rob said 205 minutes, then 205 it was—not 204, not 206. I wore my heart rate monitor, and if I was going too hard or too easy it would beep. I remember one late spring day when I was supposed to do my overdistance training for 165 minutes. I thought I'd hike really fast with a pair of ski poles and keep my heart rate up that way, but the trail I'd chosen was a tad too flat. Soon I was shuffle-jogging in my hiking boots, a kind of Groucho crabwalk that I hoped might raise my pulse. The trail got muddier, the air grew stickier, the mosquitoes bolder. At 55 minutes (a third of the way through; I became an utter ace at fractions long before the year was out) I checked my heart rate monitor—I'd been averaging only 134 beats per minute! A tick below my zone! I tried to push the pace a bit, but at the 110-minute mark I checked and my average hadn't budged. Gadzooks. For some reason I was obsessed with nudging my number up to 135, to getting it into the right range. I began to shuffle harder, sweat pouring off me, poles flapping as I ran. And by God I made it: 2 hours and 45 minutes, average heart rate 135.

In some ways it went way beyond senseless. I'd been ripping down a lovely trail, but with barely a chance to raise my gaze. I hadn't stopped to smell whatever roses there may have been, though doubtless they could smell me. I failed to feel like Joyce Carol Oates, who once wrote of running: "If there's any activity happier, more exhilarating, more nourishing to the imagination, I can't think what it might be . . . the mysterious efflorescence of language seems to pulse in the brain." Most of the words pulsing in my brain were unprintable. I knew, too, in some sane corner of my mind that there was no difference between 134 beats per minute and 135. And yet to slack off seemed to call the whole project into question. If I shaved ten minutes off today, why not cut tomorrow's workout in half? It made me a little uneasy even to entertain the thought.

On the very first morning of his run across the entire nation, as he plodded up a road from a Pacific beach, an ultra-marathoner named James Shapiro wrote that he was "losing concentration on the road as unmentionable words—'dropping out'—repeated themselves." The panic, he wrote, was familiar from his days as a Buddhist. He recalled the week-long intensive meditation period (*sesshin*) that students of Zen may choose to undertake. "There is no obligation to sit on your rear with folded legs on a black cushion from 3 a.m. to 9 p.m. with only brief respites for meals and walking. It is completely voluntary."

But you would do any of these things only if you thought they were helping you, right? It's possible that Sir Edmund Hillary really climbed Mount Everest because it was there, but for most of the hundreds who have followed the climb must have been more about *them* than about *it*. About trying to change who they were.

There was no doubt my *body* was changing. I had learned already to treat it like a machine, which was a big improvement. For most of my life I'd treated it like a houseplant, watering it when I happened to notice it, feeding it constantly whether it needed it or not. Now I tanked up with water or Gatorade before I ran, and made sure I drank three or four ounces every half hour while I worked out, and swilled some energy liquid when I was done running. "Your muscle tissues are really receptive and hungry at that point," Rob said. "For a couple of hours your body produces an enzyme that helps you replenish your energy stores. It's all about recovering quickly so you can work out again the next day." Too little glycogen—the stored energy in your muscles—and you "bonk," just run out of power; that's the rock of endurance sports. And the hard place is "blowing up"—going at such a high intensity that you produce more lactic acid in your muscles than the bloodstream can clear away. "When you blow up, you may still have energy stored in your body, but you can't get rid of the waste," said Rob. "That's why you're suddenly breathing so hard—it's not so much that you're trying to get oxygen, it's that you're trying to get rid of carbon dioxide." All the long, slow distance training should have been building up the capillary network to clear away that lactic acid; the hard uphill intervals should have been teaching my body to go harder before it started producing too much lactate. I could tell it was working. Running up hills no longer raised my heart rate so dramatically. When I lay in bed first thing in the morning and took my pulse, it was usually under 50.

But I kept circling back to the question of how this machine connected to my soul or even to my personality. As I changed the machine, was I changing the man?

If so, then the negative ways were easiest to see. I had grown more or less exercise-addicted; if some duty arose that might rob me of my daily workout, I grew tense, short-tempered, brittle. What if I got *weaker?* "I have to run every day—if I don't, I feel guilty," Joan Benoit, who won the first gold medal ever awarded in the women's Olympic Marathon, once wrote. But guilty for what? It's an obligation unlike most others. You don't owe it to anyone else, especially if you're mediocre; I couldn't even claim God had given me some talent it would be irreverent to ignore. In fact, I was ignoring my actual talents, my real obligations. But this routine was unlike most others. If you miss a few days of writing, you can make it up the next week; the works don't disappear, atrophy. If you miss a few days of training, you start again from some lower plateau. Your heart can't do quite what it was doing a week before. It's no wonder that injuries can drive athletes to despair; the time you lose will never be recovered.

Other, less-obsessed people often irritated me now. One day in early spring I went for a hike with a couple of my closest friends—a gorgeous hike, one that I love because it offers sweeping views of the island-dotted Narrows of Lake George. But I was wearing my heart monitor, and the trail wasn't all that steep, and I *was not in my zone.* I'd just read an article in one of my running magazines warning against uselessly slow "junk miles," so I kept speeding up the pace, practically running up every grade, too far ahead to chat, too restless to stop at the views. Nick hardly talked with me for the rest of the summer, and I don't blame him; I was like some guy with a new girlfriend who suddenly has no time for his buddies. Except my paramour was strapped snugly around my chest and bleated softly when I went too slowly. In the end, endurance sports are a test of yourself against yourself; they require nobody else, and sometimes they can hardly tolerate anyone else.

At other moments, though, I could almost convince myself that there was something like a meditation under way. Day after day, for instance, Rob made me practice my ski technique— slowly, without poles, exaggerating every motion. When you ski, the secret is to shift *all* your weight onto your gliding ski, to commit completely. On the one hand, you're more vulnerable way out there on one leg. With both feet solidly beneath you, or at least near the ground for quick recovery, you're not going to fall. But you're not going to soar either. A marriage, a love affair, parenthood—any relationship is safer when you stay in control, when you don't commit completely and blindly. But is it still thrilling? Skiing fast, shimming the snow, dodging around the overdressed plodders out on the track; perhaps it taught me something about playing it too safe.

For a writer—for me, anyway—commitment can be a particularly tricky issue. You spend much of your life chronicling the accomplishments of others, and you can flit from one subject to the next, avoiding the kind of engagement that forces you to deal with success and failure. I started writing sports stories for the local newspaper in junior high school, which offered an identity but not a test. (It also offered a different kind of safety; even the most bullying jock knows intuitively not to pick on the scribe who is his source of glory.) The reporter is never making the decisions—not on the pitcher's mound, or in the boardroom, or the

Oval Office. But a race, if you took it dead seriously, demanded that kind of vulnerability. *You could fail.*

Being a mediocre athlete, of course, meant I was certain to fail a good deal, at least in the eyes of those around me. I may have beaten #2009, but I was still twenty-ninth of thirty-three. In an odd way, mediocrity emerged almost as a discipline in its own right. Like most people, I've spent my life doing the things I'm good at and avoiding the rest. I had to force myself to be patient with underachievement, to get comfortable with the notion that an awful lot of other people were better at this than I was. If I was feeding my ego in certain ways, I was starving it in others, and that diet was at least as useful as my carefully calibrated intake of carbs and fiber.

Still, it was hard to *prove* it was doing me any good. No real tests came my way, no tragedies. Only the quotidian trials of living in a family with *other people* who insisted on having *their own ideas.* And those tests I failed about as often as I always had. In the end I fell back on words of Oregon track coach Bill Bowerman—the man who not only trained Steve Prefontaine but also invented the modern running shoe on his waffle iron. "Running is basically an absurd pastime on which to be exhausting oneself. But if you can find meaning in it, you can find meaning in another absurd pastime: life." At some level I simply took it on faith that Rob's regimen was prepping me for something more than skiing fast.

I just didn't know yet what it was.

# 6

"It's a World of Pain" read the sign on Ken Rundell's office wall, and the sign was right. Rundell runs the exercise physiology lab at the Olympic Training Center in Lake Placid, charged with testing and prepping the country's elite athletes. *Outside* magazine once described him as a "jowly doctor with a Gene Wilder haircut," which is more or less accurate, but painful to him (the jowly part) because he too has spent much of his life as an amateur racer. "I used to ski race, to bike," he said. "My undoing was coming here to work. They gave me a cafeteria card—all I could eat. And I gained some weight. I tried a 5K race one day, and I fell apart. I was losing to people I should not have lost to. I decided I would either lose weight, or not worry about losing races, or quit. I opted to quit." When I visited him in the spring of my training year, though, he was slowly working his way back into shape, getting ready for a masters kayaking championship.

I learned all this (and much more: Do you know about hemo-globin/myoglobin desaturation during speed skating? I do) because I was stalling. Ken Rundell is custodian of the biggest treadmill on earth ("Actually, Norway has one like this, too, but they got it after I got mine") and I was there to spend the day run-ning through his battery of tests. He'd agreed to check me out now, and to do it again in the late fall after six more months of heavy training—to give me a reading on how my body responded to this year of living strenuously.

For many years, athletes just trained as seemed best to them. No one really knew *how* to prepare the body. But the Soviet bloc, obsessed with the peculiar idea that international victories proved the superiority of their economic theories (which would have amused that aerobic powerhouse Karl M.), began to develop the science of sport. Much of what they studied was unethical and illegal—the hormone doses, the blood doping. But the athletic arms race they launched, and the realization that performance really could be researched and enhanced, gave birth to the disci-pline of sports science.

Rundell began his career as a rat man, putting rodents through their paces at Syracuse University. "I liked it," he said. "The rats didn't talk back to me. And if they did, I killed them." Still, he jumped at the chance to work on the parade of life-size animals—skiers, volleyballists, racewalkers, canoeists, lugers, ad infinitum—that pass through the Olympic Training Center each year. The drill is usually the same, a rite of passage that all aspir-ing endurance champions undergo at least once a year, and that tyros like me usually just read about in the running magazines.

First Rundell snaps you into a harness, so if you fall you'll sail into the air, not fly off the back of the treadmill. "If you did that," he explains, "you'd run right into my computers, and those are valuable." Then he clips your nose shut, straps a heart rate monitor to your chest, and hands you a large rubber mouthpiece akin to a snorkel. The mouthpiece allows you to inhale through a one-way valve, but collects all your exhalations and sends them through a tube to a computerized gas analyzer. He hits a switch, the treadmill lurches to life, and then you start to run. At first it's fairly easy: five miles per hour, six, seven, eight miles per hour. Every three minutes or so you jump off the treadmill to one side, and an assistant pricks your finger, draws a drop of blood, and runs it through another computer, checking to see how quickly lactic acid is accumulating in your system.

That's just the start, though. After about twenty minutes the finger-pricking stops and the hurt begins. The treadmill begins to speed up, and every minute the grade increases another degree. Now they're after the magic number for endurance athletes, the $VO_2$ Max. Your score tells you how well your body uses oxygen—how many milliliters of oxygen per kilogram of body weight your body can consume per minute, to be exact. In essence, that's how much energy you can produce at full bore, like an electric utility on the eighth afternoon of an August heat wave. An average person off the street would score in the 40s; the skiers who finish near the top in World Cup competitions average around 85; Daehlie, the Norwegian ski deity, reportedly tops 95, beating out the Tour de France champion Miguel Indurain by a point or two. (A thoroughbred horse would break 150.) Genetics determines most of your score; training can increase your VO2 Max by perhaps 10 percent, but choosing the right parents matters more.

VO2 Max isn't the final word. "There's no such thing as a test to tell you who'll win a race," says Rundell. "We had a guy in here who topped out at 82—he was a good skier, but he was usually beaten by a guy who scored a 67. Frank Shorter, the great marathoner, consistently tested twenty points below people he was regularly beating." Still, given two athletes with the same technique and equipment and willpower, the one with the bigger engine will win. In fact, Rundell's treadmill helps weed out those junior athletes who simply aren't worth the investment in training dollars. "Maybe we'll get a skier in here who happened to kick a good race in Junior Olympics. Maybe she picked just the right wax on a tricky day. But we get her in here and she scores a 45 on the treadmill—well, that won't buy you a hotdog in a ballpark." Even so, Rundell stresses, "We're not as strict as they are overseas. Take Germany. If their junior women aren't scoring a 65 or better they won't even look at them. If the men are under 75, they won't even look at them."

Before he can calculate your score, though, Rundell has to run you until you pretty much can't run any more. I'd made the mistake of reading John Morton's Nordic skiing novel, *Medal of Honor,* the week before, and it included a scene from a lab much like Rundell's. The hero, young Matt Johnson, shows up for his first treadmill test and watches the athlete before him go so hard that she passes out. "It happened so fast Matt almost missed it. One instant Sandy was struggling up the endless hill, the next she collapsed and the moving belt shot her off the back of the machine . . .. The rubber mouthpiece was torn free and her lip was bleeding. Several of the electrodes dangled loose." Matt's up next; by the end of the test, when the doctor cranks the treadmill to a 12 percent grade, he's barely hanging on, "straining to keep up with the carpet whisking beneath his feet." In case I thought it was just fiction, Rob, who used to run dozens of athletes on a similar treadmill, told me that when he tested the great American biath-lete Josh Thompson, he too would run till he dropped. "I'd liter-ally have to catch him coming off the back of the machine. I asked him, 'Does this happen to you in training?' 'All the time,' he said."

Needless to say, I was pretty well psyched out, and needles to say, it did begin to hurt. The treadmill was relentless; if I'd been running on a track, my body would have forced me to slack off and slow down, even a little, but here that wasn't possible. I stared straight ahead, watching Rundell, dimly aware of the numbers he was calling out. My heart rate kept climbing steadily, maxing out at 180, which was about right for my age. At one point, Rundell studied his monitor and said my VO2 score had topped "the magic 50." But that was about all I remembered hearing. "Can you give me twenty more seconds?" he asked eventually, and I said I could; I probably could have gone a minute longer, too, with the right encouragement, but I was insanely glad for an excuse to stop. When the treadmill slowed and stopped, I just sat there in a heap while someone disconnected the harness and pulled the bit from my mouth. "Your VO2 was 54.42," he said. "That's your number."

"Translated into skiing along a track," said Rob later, "this means that you have the potential to be in the top third of your age group."

"For a thirty-seven-year-old, it ain't bad," added Ken.

But it got worse. Next he tested my upper-body strength, as I pulled on a pair of cords to simulate ski poling, against a machine that stiffened the level of resistance as the test wore on. I maxed out at 230 watts, compared with an average of 254 for masters skiers (and of better than 500 for elite racers).

Then he pulled out a set of calipers and began pinching folds of fat all over my body. A few taps on his calculator, and he was able to tell me 11.7 percent of my weight was fat. "That's not too bad, but there's plenty of fat around your belly." With elite athletes it's down to 3.5 to 6.5 percent body fat.

And then, scariest of all, he put me back on the treadmill. This time, though, I was wearing roller skis—about eighteen inches of plastic with a wheel at either end, that attach to ski boots just like regular skis. Racers use them in the summertime to train on pavement, and Rundell uses them to test VO2 Max while double-poling. In other words, I was going to run the same test again, but this time with my arms instead of my legs. I'd never worn roller skis before, and to make matters even happier, a class of Skidmore College undergraduates had arrived on a field trip, so I was exhibit A. As we began, Rundell informed the crowd that American Olympian Marc Gilbertson had recently managed to keep going for twenty-four minutes on this test, pushing against the treadmill with his poles even as the slope grew ever steeper. As for me, I felt like Lucy racing the chocolate machine or Charlie Chaplin trying to keep pace with the assembly line. Within seconds I was drifting back toward the edge of the treadmill, while Rundell screamed at me to pick up the pace. I couldn't push off with my poles fast enough to keep up with the belt. After the longest two minutes of my life I finally lost the battle and fell; the harness lifted me into the air like Peter Pan, where I hung dangling poles and boots and roller skis like some hypoxic angel. "Bill's problem is in his upper body," Ken explained to the astounded undergraduates as he cut me down.

Later, at lunch, Rob looked over all my numbers and started explaining in more detail what they meant. I was more or less stuck with some, like my VO2 Max; it would go up 10 percent at best, he said. Others, like my "lactate profile"—the speed with which crippling lactic acid accumulated in my muscles—should improve more dramatically over time. One thing was certain: I needed to improve my technique and my upper body. Even if I built my engine till it was as powerful and efficient as my genetics would allow, I still needed to transmit that power to the snow.

Running, though, doesn't build those triceps and abs very precisely; once the snow melts you need to find some other way to practice that endless double-poling, and that snapping leg kick, that propel cross-country skiers. If you're an elite skier, you spend much of the summer on the Dachstein Glacier in Austria or in a special tunnel built in Finland that's filled with snow the year round. Even the top skiers, though, spend much of the summer on roller skis, the same instruments of indignity that had defeated me on the treadmill.

Imagine elongated roller skates, and you've pretty much got it, except that, as with cross-country skis your ski boots attach only at the toe, leaving the heel free, and the front wheel is ratcheted so that it can't slip back, providing the same kick as a perfect wax job. Nordic skiing on snow is the most forgiving of all sports—you don't stress your joints. And roller-skiing should be almost as good; if your knees are shot from years of jogging, roller-skiing will let you get in a workout (and a much better workout than, say, Rollerblading—the rolling resistance on inline skates is so low you don't raise your heart rate nearly as high as the kick off a roller ski, and you don't get the upper-body benefit of poles). The only nasty difference is, when you fall on skis, you slide along the snow. In the summer, friction rules. "I remember it was 1973 and I had a pair of Finnish roller skis," Len Johnson, a roller ski manufacturer, recalls. "I started down a hill I hadn't scouted. I finally realized my dog couldn't keep up with me, and my dog could run thirty miles per hour. I tried to sit back and I put my hands on the wheels, but I burned right through my gloves. Then my pants got caught in the wheels and instantly I was totally nude, just hurtling down the road.

"In those days I was importing regular roller skis, and I actually got Self magazine to do a little squib on them" says Johnson. "They said it was the hot new thing, and we got so many calls we didn't know what to do. But the first question was always, 'How do I stop?' And we had to say, 'Well, you really don't.' From a thousand inquiries we sold two pairs of skis." So Johnson invented a brake, and a binding that let you use the ski in your sneakers instead of a ski boot, and soon sales of his Nordixc were—well, not soaring. But if you hang around a heavily traveled bike path all day, you may well glimpse one or two.

And one of them might well have been me. Soon I was striding down back roads, or pumping along the shoulder of the highway on the strength of my arms and stomach, like an enormous, mobile version of those dunking toy birds that drink from the glass. If you're tired of just blending in along the jogging trail, roller skis are for you. And after an hour, the backs of your arms really ache. "By the time you come back in the fall you'll probably destroy Ken's upper-body machine," Rob told me—which seemed doubtful.

But he told me something else at that post-treadmill lunch that really did stick. I'd ordered guacamole and was just tucking in when Rob said, quietly and almost as an aside: "You know, we all like chips. But they have an awful lot of fat in them." And in that moment was born The Man Who Reads the Sides of Every

Can. "Fat has no propulsive capability," Rob continued. "It doesn't move you. When you exchange it for muscle, it's like lightening your backpack and giving yourself a little more power." It was the closest to a lecture Rob offered all year. Nearly every day when I checked my e-mail, I'd find some note from him, beginning with technique tips ("Keep your eyes focused 20-30 feet down the track") but invariably ending with a few words of encouragement. "Feel proud at how far you have come, Bill." "You are one of the most diligent people I have coached." "I can see you finding your athletic voice." Forget Vince Lombardi—I had Norman Vincent Peale coaching me. But the result was the same: total loyalty.

Anyway, dieting I could do. Heredity rules out a VO2 Max to rival Björn Daehlie's. But my DNA set no limits on how gaunt I could become; if elite skiers tested out a 7 percent body fat or less—well, that was one limbo pole I could slither under. Immediately I understood the logic of anorexic teenagers. If there's lots in your life you can't control, and one thing you can, then that one thing becomes immensely attractive. Becomes, indeed, an obsession.

Soon I was eating fat-free mayonnaise and Egg Beaters—everyone else in my aisle of the supermarket was over seventy or over three hundred. If I took Sophie out for ice cream, I ordered root beer; my own private kashrut sanctioned chicken skin and sanctified Ryvita, a kind of wafer constructed from particleboard and found on the diet shelf of your local supermarket. In early spring I went on book tour, doing ten to fifteen interviews a day to promote a new book; in city after city, the escort from the publishing company would offer to fetch me lunch, and my reply was always the same: dry bagel with lox. It's not that I stopped eating. In fact, I ate more than I've ever eaten in my life: half a pound of spaghetti for dinner, stacks of pancakes, more bananas than any six chimps. The Olympian Luke Bodensteiner, who edited a journal of one training year into his book, *Endless Winter*, recounts a typical lunch after an all-morning workout: "I started with a chocolate smoothie. Then I made myself three turkey and cheese sandwiches with everything I could find that looked like it belonged on a sandwich. I almost couldn't make them fast enough. I washed those down with three or four glasses of juice. Not satisfied, I started to boil water for spaghetti . . . My plate could hardly contain the mound I made and sure enough, as soon as I stuck my fork into it, it oozed over the side. I shoved it back onto my plate and licked the table clean like some manic hound."

But if you eat like that, and exercise like that, you lose weight anyway, especially if you're as vigilant about fat as I was becoming. I even had an eating idol: Josh Thompson, the same biathlete who ran till he dropped on Rob's treadmill. In his training book, Rob describes Thompson's roller-ski workouts: "He impressed people by double-poling on roller skis up a paved road called the Dachsteinstrasse that steadily climbs one thousand vertical meters in only five kilometers." I knew I wasn't ever going to match that. But forty pages later, Thompson also describes himself as a "fat-o-phobe, one who very carefully screens every scrap of food he puts into his mouth to make sure he's not consuming a high-fat item." That I did, and before long my pants were sliding over my hips.

What weight I kept on came from water, buckets of it. All the authorities in my fitness books were constantly insisting on hydration. I ran with a hundred-ounce bladder strapped to my back and a long tube to sip it through. I even had a chart clipped from some sports magazine that purported to show what color my urine should become if I was drinking enough (the closer to gin the better). "If you don't wake up to pee three times the night before a race, you're not drinking enough," someone at the ski tracks told me one day, and since I knew nothing about the source of this advice I followed it as gospel—there I was, at 3 a.m., groggily noting the color of the toilet bowl. My innate caution kept me from swallowing the various illicit powders, like creatine, that the locker room sages were also recommending, but I did invest in some hideously expensive Norwegian exercise drink, a kind of Scandinavian Gatorade that tasted as if it had been distilled from chalk. All in all, I spent a lot of time worrying about what was going down my throat.

And as usual I was out of step. This was right at the moment when people began to decide that healthy eating was a lot of politically correct broccoli. Even as new data was showing that 76 percent of Americans weighed more than they were supposed to (up from 54 percent in 1984), the steakhouse was coming back into vogue, and a book called *Eat Fat* was gaining respectful reviews. Leaders of the "fat acceptance" movement were appearing on all the talk shows; I'd look up from my treadmill in some far-flung gym and there would be a large and happy woman discussing how the culture had forced her to suffer through one diet after another. Those who did diet had all decided that steak was their friend. Sales of low-fat foods were dropping; even olestra, the wonder synthetic designed to let you eat all the potato chips you wanted with only the chance of "anal leakage" to show for your sins, was disappointing Procter & Gamble. I remember coming back on the airplane from a trip to Japan (where body fat is apparently taxed at a high rate) and looking wonderingly around O'Hare: Is there some kind of convention of fat people in Chicago this week? But no, it was just America—and truth be told, most of my fellow countrymen looked prosperous, content, pregnant with well-being.

The *Washington Post* published a particularly unfriendly profile of me about that time ("environmental scold," "grim," "Father Nature"). But the essayist added in this bit of personal description: "If he gained forty pounds, he'd look like a basketball player." I took it as a compliment; at least I was starting to *resemble* a cross-country ski racer. My friend John Underwood, the masters world champion at the steeplechase and the leanest person I've ever met, brought over his own personal calipers one day to test me. It was tough to find a fold to pinch. "I have bat skin," he said with just a touch of pride. "And you nearly have bat skin too."

# 7

My grandfather lived to be ninety-five—he visited Costa Rica on a banana boat when he was ninety—by walking a few brisk miles every morning and avoiding between-meals snacks. But it's not so easy any more. Here are some things you need to know if you're going to be a healthy man, according to a single issue of *Men's Health* magazine: To relieve plantar fasciitis, a painful strain in the band of ligaments running the length of your foot, roll a can of frozen orange juice back and forth under the arch of your foot; chronic, day-to-day work stress can lower your sperm count by a third; a diet rich in garlic keeps your aorta flexible; vitamin B2 fights off migraines; shrinking your waist from forty inches to thirty-seven inches cuts diabetes risk in half; you can build your triceps by doing dips off the edge of a swimming pool; if you're determined to have sex in an elevator, a spokesman for the American Elevator and Machine Corporation recommends using a freight elevator ("Many lack security cameras, but check the ceiling to make sure. Shift the control switch into neutral to stop between floors—this won't trip the alarm bell"); 42 percent of men between the ages of eighteen and forty-nine have pattern baldness; Jell-O makes the best fat-free chocolate pudding ("The other low-fat brands varied from bland to astringent, but the Jello-O hit the sweetness note right on the first spoonful"). Not only that—every night 27,000 American couples "experience a condom break or slip"; negative sit-ups can build abdominal muscles faster than crunches; you can beat pollen allergies by cutting down on outdoor activities before 10 a.m.; if you have a good friend, you're only one-third as likely to die from heart troubles as a loner; to qualify for Navy SEAL training you need to do six pull-ups and run four miles in thirty-two minutes; you may be able to bring your partner to blinding orgasm by employing an ancient Oriental pattern of nine shallow thrusts followed by one deep one, but if she cries out she may be faking because "while climaxing it's nearly impossible to exhale." Also this: Make sure to have your summer clothing pressed at the dry cleaner ("You'll be the crisp standout in a crowd of wrinkles"); buy red grapes because they contain "reservatrol, the same substance in wine that supposedly offers heart-protecting benefits" and then freeze them to use as ice cubes in cocktails; if the bench press machine is in use at your gym, substitute a step push-up; if you want to win your girlfriend a stuffed animal at the fair, you will need to strike the *front edge* of the target on the strongman machine with the sledgehammer; only flatter your date once an evening because "every compliment after the first one takes away half the value of the compliment that preceded it." And, of course, this: Nine hundred men in south Wales were asked to record how often they ejaculated—after ten years the most sexually active man had a 50 percent lower mortality rate.

For a long time—say, three or four million years—being a woman was hard work. But beginning in about 1985, manhood became nearly as time-consuming. The training begins early— some of the new GI Joe action figures, for instance, boast larger biceps than waists. Look at a sample year of *Men's Fitness*, a young men's magazine poised halfway on the spectrum that runs from the hard-core bodybuilding rags to the classy operations like *Men's Journal*. Just to judge from the covers, there are "24 ways to customize your physique," "six dangerous foods," "12 instant nutrition fixes," "seven best biceps builders," "Better sex—10 ways to drive them insane," "Is she nuts?—4 danger signs," "play dirty and win—13 head games," "ten most overrated foods," "7 super shakes for peak energy," "5 awesome back wideners," "20 crucial golf skills," "5 ready-made seduction dates," "20 hospital survival tips," "6 moves for bigger arms," "fuel her fire—10 hot tips," "39 things to never do" ("never perform abdominal move- ments in a fast or uncontrolled way"), and "50 Ways to Improve Your Life—Guaranteed." Every cover shows a man with wash- board abs ("in fifteen minutes a day"); every article is written in the same breathless tone; and every issue features ads for video series on how to make love more proficiently, enlarge your penis ("electric or manual systems"), and reupholster your head.*

I'd never read these kinds of magazines before, because I grew up in the last easy days for guys. It's true that being a weenie was no fun, but that was mostly because of the gym teachers; none of the guys I knew in high school took steroids; in college "wardrobe"

---

*Life has gotten harder for women, too, who are required to be not just gorgeous but fit. For example, one women's sports magazine I saw provided tips on remedying beauty tragedies like the "helmet hair" often experienced by bikers. (Blow-dry your hair in an inverted position to "confuse the roots.")

meant "jeans." Certainly muscles were no huge deal. I'd never systematically lifted weights before Rob handed me my schedule, which included three weekly strength workouts along with all the running and roller-skiing. For the first few days, I was improvising—he had me load encyclopedias into a backpack and then lunge or jump; for my arms I did push-ups. But soon he'd sent me one of his inventions—the sliding-seat Vasa Trainer, which is used mainly by swimmers, but is perfectly designed for cross-country ski training. I was faithful to it—endless sets of crunches and bicep curls and tricep extensions—and before much time had passed muscles actually began to appear on my formerly smooth body. And soon thereafter, vanity began to infect my formerly oblivious consciousness. I found myself posing in front of mirrors as I shaved—flexing my pecs so they'd pop up and down, tensing my butt (my *glutes*, I mean) when I showered, feeling the indentations in my upper arm that marked the birth of my triceps. You couldn't really *make out* my washboard abs, but I could count the ridges of muscle like ribs whenever I tightened my stomach.

Previously, Arnold Schwarzenegger had always struck me as the silliest of men—repulsive, almost. But now I read his autobiography, *Arnold*, with new understanding. "It was the summer I turned 15 . . . Seeing new changes in my body, feeling them, turned me on . . . It was the first time my mind knew my thighs, calves, and forearms were more than just limbs." He soon learned "that pain meant progress. Each time my muscles were sore from a workout, I knew they were growing," Arnold writes. "When I went to the gym I got rid of every alien thought in my mind. I tuned in to my body as if it were a musical instrument. In the dressing room I would start thinking about training, about every body part, what I was going to do, how I was going to pump up."

For a while he worked as a personal trainer, but it quickly sickened him: "People who would never benefit from what I had to give kept taking my time. They paid and came to the gym, but it was a disgusting, superficial effort on their part. They merely went through the motions, doing sissy workouts, pampering themselves."

Though Arnold would have giggles over my workouts (and my muscles), I felt a little of what he had felt: "My self-confidence grew as I saw how much control I was gaining over my body. In two or three years I'd actually been able to change my body entirely. That told me something—if I could change my body that much, I could also, through determination and discipline, change anything else I wanted."

But Arnold, by turning bodybuilding from a sweaty, slightly sad subculture into mainstream entertainment, doubtless did more to undermine self-confidence than pump it up. He offered a new standard, one that in slightly less grotesque form soon stared out at men from billboards and magazine ads. I have a friend my age, divorced once, whom we always teased for working hard on his arms in the gym. "You married guys don't understand," he'd say with a grin. "Women today don't just want a nice guy. They want the whole package." As Susan Faludi puts it in her recent book, *Stiffed*, men are increasingly independent agents in an "ornamental culture," measured by the size of their portfolios, their SUVs—and their quads and pecs. Or, in Arnold's words, "I felt there was more to life than just plodding through an average existence. I'd always been impressed by stories of greatness and power. Caesar, Charlemagne, Napoleon were names I knew and remembered. I wanted to be something special, to be recognized as the best."

Only one person at a time gets to be Mr. Universe, though. Some of us are ectomorphs—"a thin person with a light bone structure and long tenuous muscles," according to Arnold's glossary. "The ectomorph has a tough time gaining weight and building strength." And, as later emerged, Arnold, along with his fierce Teutonic will and endomorphic genes, also gobbled steroids.

The obsession with muscle, in fact, could pretty easily become a pathology. Some years after Arnold's autobiography launched a thousand gyms, Sam Fussell wrote *Muscle*, a much more dystopian account. It begins with him as a lanky, bookish, extremely scared resident of New York City: "My days I spent running wide-eyed in fear down city streets"; at night he triple-locked the door to his sublet, nailed his windows shut, drew his shades. He was almost as much a cartoon character as the bulging Schwarzenegger. But then he found himself drawn to the Y and to the world of lifting. Soon he was eating endlessly so that he could build more muscle, and spending half his workday in the office bathroom with his shirt off admiring his new armature. "As I flexed, I saw veins larger than tug ropes spring up from nowhere to lace my biceps and triceps, now clearly delineated. My forearms, once celery stalks, were now bowling pins." His friends (he'd been to Oxford, for heaven's sake) talked about upcoming books and new indie films; "I sternly lectured them on maximum protein utilization."

Eventually, nothing but his muscles mattered. Fussell quit his job and journeyed to southern California, mecca of bodybuilding, where he found a home in the Shangri-La gym and a mentor named Bamm Bamm, a steroids pusher who had so disorganized his body with drugs and iron that he had to wear a diaper when he worked out. The most memorable set piece in his book involves

Fussell's attempt to make love to a similarly carapaced female builder; it's like two Chevy Suburbans trying to mate. Even in his excess, though, Fussell wasn't so far from the cultural mainstream: "The television in our living room showed bodybuilders in commercials, in sitcoms, even in game shows . . . Every beer advertisement seemed to have one of the diseased pumping weights in the background. And in the magazines and newspapers, the models in their underwear no longer languorously lounged in *contra posto*. Now they 'stood relaxed' with sharply defined abdominal muscles and blooming pectorals."

Fussell finally competed in a contest. He came in second, but he clearly wasn't going to be the next Schwarzenegger—and finally something snapped. "Having come three thousand miles, having gained eighty pounds, I wanted out—out of that body, out of that mind, that regimentation . . . I felt that if you could somehow find a chink in my armor and pry apart a muscular pauldron from a gorget, you'd find nothing in that vast white empty space but a tiny soul about the size of an acorn."

To an ectomorph like me, his warnings were pretty unnecessary. The veins in my arms bulged like phone cords, not tug lines; my forearms bloomed from celery stalks to broccoli stalks; my wife was the only one to notice I was sprouting muscle mass, and even she, in my opinion, paid far too little attention to the details of my emergent triceps. Before I got too far gone, though, I finished a workout in a gym in some strange city and then noticed a vending machine by the exit. It sold cans of Ripped Force, a "hyperthermogenic," "high-tech," "energy-producing" drink, a "state of the art blend formulated to increase thermogenic delivery for a ripped, defined physique." By now I was reaching for my quarters. "You've spent hours in the gym trying to build muscle

mass," the label cooed. "The time has come to show it off." I
spent the next two days doubled over with stomach cramps; when
I actualled read the ingredients, it turned out to feature *ma buang,*
a Chinese herb that's high in ephedrine. Among many other
things, it purged me of some of my burgeoning muscle fever.

Endurance athletes, in fact, are not supposed to Popeye up—
more muscle takes more blood to feed it, eventually reducing your
efficiency. But since I was spending too much time in gyms, I got
to watch the iron tribe at close range in their natural habitat, and
their every attitude was simply an engorged version of my own.

Their philosophy lite, for instance—if you listen to two bodybuilders for sixty seconds, one or the other is bound to offer a
profundity. Sometimes they talk to themselves. I remember sitting
on a bench in a Niagara Falls gym doing my leg extensions; a few
feet away, a massive fellow in a tank top was running the stack on
the bench press machine. In between reps, to no one in particular,
he would repeat, "If you're not *hurting,* you're not *progressing,*
you're *regressing.*" Clang, the weights would crash down. "If
you're not *hurting . . .*"

For all their straining bulk, bodybuilders possess a certain
daintiness, too. One enormous specimen climbed out of a squat
rack, lumbered over to the mirrored wall that encircled the gym,
and primly lifted the hem of his shorts an inch or so to check out
the precise contours of some new thigh muscle he was developing;
his delighted expression matched perfectly my daughter's face
when she first painted her toenails.

As the year wore on, I began to notice and admire muscle in
ways I hadn't before—functional muscle, propelling the miniscule
proportion of the workforce that hasn't become brains on sticks.
We went to the Big Apple Circus in mid-summer and sat in the

front row, close enough that the horses scattered sawdust on our laps as they galloped by. And close enough that you could watch biceps straining, deltoids stretching, hamstrings starting to quiver. On our annual trip to Lincoln Center for *The Nutcracker* that December, I found myself looking past the smiling gracefulness of the ballerinas for the athletic struggle underneath—the calves and quads that were starting to shake by the end of a long pas de deux, the spring-loading step before the jeté.

No matter how many ballerinas I watched, though, the subtle equation of strength with masculinity never completely vanished from my mind. On most weight-lifting machines, you determine the resistance by sticking a pin somewhere in a stack of ten-pound weights. If you have to move the pin down the stack to reach your level, it means that you are stronger than the person who used the machine before you; if you have to move it up, it means you're weaker. As the year went on, I found myself in the middle of the pack at most gyms, and then maybe a little ahead—I was moving the pin down! Not that it meant anything, except to my own self-image.

But self-image matters, I was finding out. As a boy, resolutely unphysical, I supposed I should exercise in order to get girls. I got girls anyway; eventually I got married and fathered a child and so fulfilled my genetic mandate, and the fact that I couldn't reliably open pickle jars did not prevent my DNA from passing down yea unto the generations. And yet did I measure up to my forebears, those sturdy small-town westerners? Growing up, Dad had spent his summers at a tiny log cabin on the edge of Mount Rainier—a place without lights or running water, in the shadow of the great Douglas firs. We'd visit the cabin every few years on some vacation driving trip, and usually we'd find my cousin Craig there—a mountaineer, he was forever heading off to Pakistan or Baffin Island or some other place with high icy cliffs to conquer. Sometimes he'd open his pack to show us his collection of carabiners, pitons, and ropes. Dad loved it—this was his fantasy life long before Everest mania. But he'd reared *us* in the cushy suburbs of the East; sometimes it seemed to me as if I was devolving, defying Darwin. Perhaps that explains my willingness to push and pull stacks of iron in sweat-soaked gymnasiums while "Eye of the Tiger" blared on the tinny p.a.

That summer Mom and Dad celebrated their fortieth anniversary. We all joined them at a slightly down-at-the-heels resort in the White Mountains that offered a shaggy nine-hole golf course out back. I'd never played golf—it seemed Republican to me, and it seemed rich with opportunities for embarrassment. But it was a great pleasure that summer to head out there with my dad and my brother. I had no swing; they had to show me how to grip the club. But when I connected I had power—the ball would sail away into the middle distance. It didn't bother me that it went left or right or onto the neighboring fairway. I just liked the idea that it went long and strong.

# 8

Coaches stood on stepladders in the gym, hurling volleyballs down at girls who sprawled across the floor to dig them out; Greco-Roman wrestlers, short and intense, prowled the weight room on the balls of their feet; in the always-open cafeteria, where red and blue Powerade bubbled in the coolers instead of soda, kayakers listened to a coach outline the day's program in some Iron Curtain accent: "If it's lightning out today, den you vill paddle faster."

Lake Placid's Olympic Training Center, where I'd done my treadmill testing in the spring, is one of three such facilities in the country. National teams, and development teams of promising young stars, rotate through for their training camps—on any given week, biathletes, rifles strapped to their backs, might share the dorms with racewalkers or archers or powerlifters. "It's sports Disney World," says Tracy Lamb, who runs the operation for the U.S. Olympic Committee, an aristocratic court of the cardiovascular elite, a kingdom from which flab and sloth have been banished. The rooms are Spartan, like state college dorms, and when the clock strikes eleven the place falls into utter silence, the deep quiet of extremely tired people who know it all starts again when they awake.

I'd been invited up to join a group of young endurance runners for a weekend camp. They were just high school kids—regional champions, but nowhere near the international caliber of most of the other athletes on hand from other sports. Their mere presence indicated the sort of desperation that currently grips endurance sports in this country. Americans still win the most Olympic medals—many years they own the swimming pool, the women's soccer pitch, the ice rink, the sprinter's straightaway; always they hold their own in the gymnasium, on the downhill course, along the rowing lake, even in the show jumping ring. But in the endurance sports—in the ski marathons of the winter and the running races that last longer than two minutes—the Yanks are no longer even a factor. Explanations abound, many of them eugenic or cultural: Kenyans and Ethiopians live at high altitude, they grow up running to school, they have no other route to success, hence they can run forever. (Some American road races have even started to reserve prize money for Americans; their sponsors apparently believed it was unhelpful to the cause of merchandising to have anonymous Africans win year after year—in the words of one sportscaster, "They won't do stand-up.") These are terrific theories, explaining everything except the lack of a Tibetan marathon squad, and the fact that a Brazilian who grew up at sea level dropped the world marathon mark by an astounding forty-five seconds in 1998. Also, when Nike decided to train two top Kenyan runners for cross-country skiing at the Nagano

Games, they went about exactly half as fast as the Norwegians, a race somewhat whiter than typing paper. (To be fair, the Africans had skied for only a year. "On the big downhills, our skis were going so fast," said Mike Boit. "We found ourselves going directly in the bushes.")

John Underwood, a local endurance guru who had organized the Lake Placid camp, blames the poor American results on something quite different: a lack of organization. "We have two million high school runners," he says. "That's our talent pool—it's like a tenth as big as the total population of Kenya. That's plenty." What we lack, he insists, is a national system to identify and then train the standouts. "A lot of the high school coaches, when the kids come in at 3 p.m. and say, 'What are we going to do today?' he'll say, 'I don't know—what do you want to do?' You have to start out knowing what to do, otherwise you'll spend ten years wasting your time. So at a camp like this we can say: Here's how much you should be training, here's how hard, here's what you should be eating."

Americans have long been wary of any national sports program. Picking the elite and training them hard reminds us of the Soviet sports schools or the East German academics with their doped-up cyborgs. Instead, we've followed an entrepreneurial model, with each athlete as a little start-up company. Most American sports federations make it their main business to conduct trials every Olympic year, and whoever happens to win constitutes our squad. Letting the cream rise may work out for sprinters—"you can train for eighteen months, and if you have the talent you can medal," says Underwood—but endurance athletes have to build steadily for more than a decade before they reach their peak sometime after twenty-five. By the time

European skiers reach, say, junior high, they're already following the rough outline of a national training schedule: Coaches
have agreed on a master plan of about how much work is needed
at each age. And as long as the athletes keep showing promise,
the national team supports them. But in this country, save perhaps for four short years on a college scholarship, endurance
athletes are mostly on their own.

The result has been a collapse in American distance running
unlike anything that's ever been seen in our sports culture. First,
other nations pulled ahead of us on the international scene; then
even within the country, as athletes began to lose hope and interest, times began to slow. It's not just that the Kenyans are getting
faster than we are; it's that the Kenyans are speeding up while we
are slowing down. "In 1980, I coached a guy at Eugene, Randy
Melancon, who ran a 28:20 for the 10K," says Bill Freeman, a
sports scientist who has been helping run the Lake Placid camp."
That 28:20 would have been about the twenty-fifth best time in
the United States that year. If he'd run the same time seventeen
years later, in 1997, it would have been the second fastest of the
season." George Regan, regional director of the U.S.A. Track and
Field, the sports governing body, adds, "We haven't hit bottom
yet. I don't see any turnaround. If we started doing everything
right today, it would still take us ten years to produce the next
world-class Olympians. That's two more Olympiads. We can't
even hope until 2010."

Thus, this squad of high schoolers running in the cold rain of
an Adirondack summer. They did lap upon lap around John
Brown's farm, where freed slaves had once worked the fields; they
listened to talks on nutrition; they calculated training plans for
the years ahead. It was, in many ways, a pedestrian experience.

The two coaches I roomed with could and did spend hours discussing how many pairs of cut-rate Tiger sneakers one had been able to score at a going-out-of-business sale, or the fascinating setup the other had devised to let him video a half hour of his feet on the treadmill in an effort to make sure his heel strike was technically sound. These people were in it for the long haul, ready to contemplate a decade of two-a-day training runs.

All the more fascinating, then, how often the talk turned from the physiology of endurance to the psychology, from the heart and lungs to the mind and soul. I already knew that for me, stuck in the middle of the pack, every race was about deciding if I wanted to push and hurt or not. But the same issue seemed to haunt the folks up front as well. Even though Bill Freeman appears to have been born with a stopwatch around his neck, even though he recalls people by their times, as in "He was a 3:53:6 miler," even though he wrote a book called *Peaking When It Counts*, full of meticulous charts designed to produce championship performances at the right moment—this same Bill Freeman nonetheless told me over lunch that "most of the developments at the high end in the future will be in sports psychology. People simply can't train more than they are now. We've seen the limits. As early as the 1970s, we had one national-caliber runner who was running 350 miles a week for a while. That's fifty miles a day. Who's going to train more than that? We're backing down from the megamileage—even 130 miles a week makes us wonder. And that's where sports psychology comes in. We need to develop the same kind of mental profile of what it takes to succeed as we've done with the physiological. With an awful lot of athletes that's the shaky thing."

I'd already come across plenty of sports psychology books.

There was *Inner Skiing*, for instance, in the same series with *Inner Tennis* and *Inner Golf*. Dedicated to the guru Maharaj Ji, it encourages readers to be like baby birds who never doubted they would learn to fly and so were soon able to "soar on currents of air, to dive, turn and glide." Or Terry Orlick's *In Pursuit of Excellence*, which reminds us that "once we gain control of our inner world, competition need not be the fear trip that it has been for some people." Like all self-help authors, the sports psychologists share a fervent belief in the powers of visualization, of goal-setting, of focus, and they share the same soft, bland vocabulary too. I'd never been impressed. But now I was trying something harder than I'd tried before—to keep my concentration even when it started to hurt. And so I began paying more attention.

That night the high school runners gathered to listen to Tracy Lamb, who coached the American and Canadian biathlon squads before he took over Olympic Training Center. He began with the usual stuff: Visualize the course, run the race over and over in your mind, write down your targets over and over till they're a part of you, set a goal for each practice. He spieled well, though, and soon the whole room was silent save for the occasional random beep from someone's Timex Triathlon. "We all get nervous before a race," he said. "It's not normal to put a bib on. But you can react to that nervousness in a couple of ways. One is to go into your comfort zone. Maybe you look around at the other competitors and pick where you'll finish: 'I can beat *him*, I can beat *him*, uh oh, I *can't* beat him. If I just do what I'm supposed to do everyone will be happy with me.' That's psychologically secure. But we want to expand the comfort zone, and to do that you can't be afraid of failing." In other words, if you run the first three kilometers thirty seconds faster than you've run them before, you may end up with a breakthrough time, and you may fall apart on the last 2K and need to crawl home. "If you're going to expand your comfort zone, you're going to fall on your keister pretty often," said Lamb. "And if you just keep it in that safe zone, you're going to go through life living in suburbia, and you'll never know what's in your heart and soul."

Success, of course, is relative; for some people it means working up the courage to enter a race and then gutting it through to the finish, no matter how far behind; for others it means setting a new world record. I knew already that for me, consigned to the middle of the pack, it was less tangible: Would I go as hard as I possibly could, enduring the hurt, or would I settle for a little less, a reasonable effort over a long distance that would be just as impressive to my friends when I told them about it later? When I'd begun my workouts, I hadn't figured out that subtle distinction; I reckoned that merely getting strong enough to finish, say, the 58K Birkebeiner would be enough. But now I had a race with myself, to exceed my own natural limits. *"Smart people, normal people, when it starts hurting, what do they do?"* Lamb asked. *"They stop. Are you normal people? No. When it starts to hurt, you think, I've got to go a little harder."* All the kids nodded, wide-eyed, eager to test themselves.

I wasn't so eager. Growing older, it seemed to me, usually involved figuring out how *not* to risk your ego, how not to put yourself on the line. You found that comfort zone, that suburbia of the mind and heart, and you stayed safely inside it. Journalism, as I said before, allows its practitioners to stay in the comfort zone more than most jobs. Unlike the people we write about—politicians, entrepreneurs, athletes—we don't have to ultimately commit to something. We write about Al Gore, and then the next day we write about George W. Bush, while Al Gore has to go on being Al Gore every day, and either winning or losing. It's not that journalism's easy—it's as hard to do well in as any other serious craft. It's just that barring sloppiness or laziness it's difficult to *fail*. And the unwritten rules of this craft discourage even an emotional involvement with the subject: You aren't supposed to care whether Al Gore or George W. wins. Even your heart is not supposed to be out on the line. It's like running a 10K race at a nice, even pace, not pushing yourself, not taking the risk you'll blow up. Forty-five minutes every time out.

That psychology started to change when I began writing books, an almost athletic endeavor. In the first place, you commit yourself fully to some subject or argument, spend years with it, force yourself to believe in its inherent importance. And when you are finally finished and ready to publish your effort, it enters a competition as brutal as anything in sport. There are reviews—cheers or boos, just like at the stadium. And there are statistics, too, reams of them. Not just the bestseller lists, but all the data the publisher collects—they can tell you by the day how you're doing. (And for the truly masochistic author, Amazon.com can tell you by the second exactly what you rank compared to every author in the English-speaking world. You're 14,535th today. But don't feel too bad—Herman Melville is 23,879th.)

Not only that, but your publisher sends you out on book tour too. As the snow was melting that spring, while I was making the transition from the ski tracks to the running trails, the time arrived for me to go on the road in support of a book I'd written about population. It was called *Maybe One*, an argument for smaller families, and it represented a couple of years of hard work. The tour began successfully enough: I got through *Good*

*Morning America* without picking my nose, though I was followed immediately by the first clips from the new movie *Godzilla*, whose roars doubtless erased my two minutes of answers from the American mind. From there I headed off to seventeen cities in fourteen days, clutching my sheaf of airline tickets and my endless, evergrowing fax list of appointments. Whatever city I woke up in, I was staring at a microphone by six-thirty, grinning my way through some FM chat with Mike'n'Dave, the Morning Monsters, or Tom'n'Liza, Keepers of the PIX 106 Breakfast Zoo. On to Daybreak Cleveland and a quick interview before this week's dogs from the animal shelter appeared, begging to be adopted. That's how *I* felt—won't someone take me home and look out for me? A few rounds of combative talk radio, perhaps a peaceful interlude with a public radio reporter who had actually read the book, an hour or two on the treadmill, and then it was time for The Reading. Most nights some local bookstore asks you to recite half an hour's worth of your deathless prose; each evening, therefore, you have to worry if you'll draw a crowd or face stoically the small humiliation of ranking somewhere beneath the last eight authors to come through town, each of whom managed to fill the folding chairs.

Usually folks would appear to hear me speak, but usually they were clutching old books of mine they wanted me to sign, relics of other, more successful book tours. The stench of failure began to cling to this jaunt, deepening as it went on. I remember waking up at four one morning to do a phone interview with the radio host working the graveyard shift at a Denver talk station.

"What's with this book about kids?" he demanded. "Are you still married?"

"Me?" I asked groggily.

"No, the telephone. Of course you, you idiot," he said. Of course.

When I actually got out of bed that morning, I made the rounds of Miami rock stations, taping shows that would appear in the wee hours of Sunday morning. "This is the Planet Earth show, and I'm Terry, your spaceship navigator," said one host. "This is Power to the People, on Power 96," said the next, and so it went. The Warner Brothers TV affiliate interviewed me for *their* Sunday morning book show, cleverly titled *Between the Lines*. "We do a one share," the host admitted. "But the government says we need it to protect our license." By the end of the day I was in Minneapolis, for some reason booked to give a reading at the planetarium. Jupiter swam overhead as I used a glowstick to make out my text, entertaining a grand total of six who had crowded under the dome.

I am not saying this was hard work, like designing software or collecting tolls. It's a price well worth paying for the privilege of getting to write books. But the sense of being out on the line, of risking humiliation, was, as always, intense. As it happened, I was spending my plane flights reading *A False Spring*, one of the best books about failure that I'd ever come across. Pat Jordan, the author, signs out of high school as a pitcher for the Milwaukee Braves organization. After a few early successes in the farm system, he begins to struggle. He watches the players who have been cut from the minor league camps: "They slid their suitcases out from underneath their cots and filled them quickly with their belongings, the small space around their cot suddenly bare and soon to be filled by the belongings of some new player in camp. They moved in quick silence so as not to wake any of the others, who would then be witness to their humiliation." Jordan wonders if maybe he should have stopped with his memories of high school glory intact, like some of his contemporaries who had rejected the scouts "rather than gamble for a far riskier but more gratifying success." The thought of "continued and maybe permanent failure terrified me," he writes. "I had avoided failure so much longer than most (all those years of no hitters and strikeouts) that its intrusion into my life was at first incomprehensible and then so terrifying that I would do anything to shake it. I was even willing to compromise the only thing in my life I had ever consciously cultivated, and the only thing I had ever consciously valued—my natural talent." He changes his pitching style, sinks further, slinks away. Abject.

Writers aren't as naked as pitchers—if your book doesn't sell you can blame your publisher for not supporting it, you can pat yourself on the back for being just a little too far ahead of the curve, you can even place your hope in posterity. (Posterity never rehabilitated a losing pitcher.) Still, by the end of the book tour, or after a particularly unpleasant review ("He is irritating not only because he is so wrong, but because he is so sanctimonious"—*The New Republic*), the temptation to find some other way to spend your life can grow strong.

Which is why it always amazes me that adults might voluntarily pursue endeavors that offer the real risk of failure. Like training hard, day after day, to run long races. John Underwood, who was running the Lake Placid camp, sat down in the cafeteria one night to tell his own story over a glass of anti-freeze-blue Powerade. After growing up as a cross-country ski racer in the Adirondacks, he'd gone off to college to run; he'd been a national-caliber steeplechaser, but never at the absolute top. Following college he'd coached a highly successful Nordic ski program at an Oregon college, but after various run-ins with the authorities he'd given it all up, moved to upstate New York, went to work in a lumberyard, and started a family. "When I was thirty-eight I decided to get back in shape. I hadn't run a running race in nine years." He found a coach in Bill Freeman, the sports science authority, who tailored a program to his schedule. Within a year he ran a 9:45 steeplechase, about a minute off his college best. And then he committed to his goal, winning the World Masters Championship the next season. "I trained real hard, and by the day of the race I was able to say to myself, Of all the races I've ever trained for, this is the best-prepared I'd ever been. I said, Johnny, you've got to concentrate for nine minutes and then it's over." By the final backstretch, as they cleared the last water barrier, he was in a lead pack of four. "I said to myself, This is it, you can get nothing, a medal, or a win. I just flew; I opened up four seconds on them down the stretch. It was the greatest victory in thirty years of racing. It finally came out the way it was supposed to."

It's worth noting that this was essentially a private victory. The world barely notices the *Olympic* steeplechase champion; the sport's only exposure at the last Games came when a trailing American decided to amuse the crowd with a vault *into* the water pit. The forty-year-old steeplechase champion of the World *Masters* Games is slightly more prominent than the employee-of-the-month at the Shop'N'Save. No, his triumph had nothing to do with fame and everything to do with the fact that down that last stretch he *went* when he could have eased up. And it is a victory (or a failure) equally available to the less genetically endowed stuck in the middle of the pack. As with writing a book, exactly one person knows if you've given it your best shot, or if you've been satisfied with something less.

Later that day I stood next to Freeman as he clicked the stopwatch on a long train of high school runners. "I remember reading an article in *Runner's World* where they interviewed a lot of marathoners," he said. "They asked, 'What do you think about when you're racing?' Well, the people they interviewed were mostly dinks. People were saying things like 'I mentally build a house.' That's pretty much how you define an unimportant athlete. He may forget his pain and discomfort, but he's just hopping around out there. Rest assured that when Frank Shorter was winning marathons, he was not building a house in his head. He was thinking about his heart rate, his breathing, what the other athletes are doing."

He had withdrawn, this is, into that space of almost-timeless calm and focus, that flow state I'd discovered a few times already as some race-within-a-race became all absorbing. A state sweet enough that it made the psychic risk of failure worthwhile. I wanted back there. But winter was still six months away.

## 9

Of both the English-language cross-country skiing novels, I like John Morton's *Medal of Honor* the very best. (Doubtless Norwegian libraries have shelves full of Nordic romances and cross-country science fiction, but the only other English novel I know in this micro-genre is Kevin Hayes's *Kickland*, which hinges on the discovery of a new formula for glide wax.) *Medal of Honor* opens with the hero, Matt Johnson, near the end of a training run up a mountain near his New Hampshire home:

> If he were running from a grizzly, Matt couldn't have pushed himself any harder. He was red-lining, sustaining his heart rate at the highest level possible. Demanding more of his body would produce total collapse . . .
>
> "Stop the pain," cried an inner voice, "back off, no one will ever know. The Olympics are a fantasy made for television . . ."
> As he slogged across the rocky saddle leading to the summit, his pulse drowned out all other sounds, and his legs moved

only by memory. He staggered on, pushing through the young balsams, finally reaching the steel tower at the peak, where he bent over, gasping for air and fumbling with the tiny button on his digital watch.

59:47!

"All right!" he yelled to the surrounding evergreens. "First time under an hour!"

The book unfolds in prescribed fashion: Young Matt makes the biathlon team despite a jealous teammate who tries to sabotage his rifle; he shows great promise of winning America's first medal in the sport; and then he has to decide whether to donate blood to save the life of the (doped-up) Russian champion, thus costing him his bid for gold. Also there's a Norwegian girl in a sauna and a lot of tasty descriptions of ski waxing ("If I were racing today, I might give Rex Blue a try. It might slide better in the higher humidity.")

For American cross-country skiers, though, the most moving parts of the book are probably the descriptions of ski races in Europe; or, more specifically, the descriptions of the giant crowds that fill the stadiums and line the courses three deep, ringing cowbells and screaming encouragements as the skiers power up hills. While Matt waits to start his first World Cup race, a Canadian competitor fills him in: "Here in Germany the only sport more popular on TV is soccer . . . But just remember, Matt, these Europeans put their pants on one leg at a time, just like we do!"

Well, yes. But they get huge endorsements for *wearing* their pants, their shirts, their jackets, their toques. The question is, why do Europeans care about this kind of sport, or why do Americans not?

I was rereading *Medal of Honor* on a midsummer plane flight west to Oregon, where the glacier on the slopes of Mount Hood stays skiable all year long. I was on my way to ski on snow for the first time in months, but more to the point I was on my way to ski with Ben Husaby, one of the great American racers in the era since Bill Koch. Twice an Olympian, he'd survived for years by reselling some of the skis his sponsors gave him each year. Now, nearing retirement, he worked in a Bend, Oregon, auto body while he studied to become a teacher. The closest he'd come to fame was a brief appearance in a Snickers commercial.

Husaby turned out to be Bunyanesque, a complete contrast to most of the lissome and willowy racers I'd met before. And he turned out to be gregariously friendly and introspectively insightful all at once. We wandered up the glacier looking for a level patch to ski. The best we could do was about seventy-five feet, back and forth, which was actually okay since the altitude had me by the chest. We worked on balance for a while (he skied two hundred yards straight down the slope on one ski, the other leg stretched out behind him like some giant northern stork); we worked on glide; and then we wandered down to the lodge at the bottom of the hill and spent the afternoon talking.

"I grew up in Minnesota hunting rabbits on skis with my bow and arrow," he said. "I started when I was seven. My parents weren't really in a position to afford a lot of things, but they went to Eastern Mountain Sports and got me skis." By his senior year in high school, he'd won a couple of junior titles, and the national team asked if he wanted to go to Europe. "I remember thinking, I'll miss five weeks of school, but then I thought of the opportunity. And when I got over there . . . well, I had no idea this stuff existed, the World Cup tour and all that."

Husaby was hooked, and spent the next decade delaying adulthood, training year after year, always tantalizingly close to international success, but never close enough. "Every year there would be at least one of us Americans who's finishing in the top twenty-five at races. God, you're less than fifty seconds behind the best over thirty kilometers. You think, on a good day with the right skis I'm capable of making the jump. I remember my first time at the Holmenkollen in Oslo, the most famous fifty-kilometer course in the world. I was twentieth place after thirty-five kilometers. I remember feeling so awesome. And then I hit the wall—it was euphoric and disheartening at the same time."

Being a Nordic ski racer in America, he said, "is like being lost in subdivision. You think your mental training, your fitness, is on the right track, but then you find you are in a cul-de-sac. There's no Oddvar Brå [a proto-Daehlie] to say, 'We tried that in the early seventies; it's good as far as it goes, but here's the limiting factor.' Some of the views from the subdivision are nice, and I kept thinking I was getting closer, but . . ." Like some karmalocked Hindu, he kept repeating the cycle. "For a lot of the time it was the only life I knew. There was some security in the uncertainty of it all. Even in June you know that the first week of January is going to be an important week: the nationals. You become addicted to the cycles. The fun of April when you take a break, the pain of May when you start training again, the fluidity of the summer months, the excitement of waiting for snow, and then the defining months of winter."

As we talked, we watched the crowds boarding the chairlift for the trip up to the slopes. There were plenty of downhill ski racers. Mount Hood, which salts its slopes each day so that they'll freeze hard overnight, is the traditional summer training ground for the alpine crowd. But there were also scads of snowboarders, some with boom boxes, all with the sunglasses of the moment, the right jackets, the practiced slouch. "There were a few of us who spent the last ten years trying to make cross-country skiing a bit cooler," said Husaby. "We were listening to the right music, wearing the right clothes, the right sunglasses. But it doesn't do much good if no one's paying attention.

"The timing is right and wrong for a thing like cross-country skiing," he continued, and indeed for any of the endurance sports. "It's right because kids are beginning to realize material life is not so key. They've seen their parents work for the three cars, the ten-day vacation to Cabo once a year, the whole shitty life. But the kids aren't picking it up from a struggle angle. They don't understand that perseverance is a rite of passage—the whole Hemingway thing. Struggle is equated with bad. The most gain for the least output is good."

I asked him how he'd sell the sport if CBS let him direct the cross-country ski coverage for the next Olympics. "You can talk forever about how hard we train and all that, and people still don't get it. It's like on another planet. But I'd try to draw comparisons. The average running marathon has a climb of six hundred feet, while a cross-country skiing marathon may climb six thousand feet. I would show the speed, make comparisons people can understand. I'd shoot it from a snowmobile so they'd get an idea what the speed really is. There should be graphics showing the pitches, and showing them in comparison to roads people know about—The Road to the Sun at Glacier Park, for instance. Look, a 6 to 7 percent grade is really steep for a road, but we have plenty of hills in a race that are 15 or 20 percent. And I'd compare it to a commute, Boston to New York, say. I'd show how it wouldn't take us much longer to do it on skis than it does to do it in a car."

All of which makes sense, but all of which misses the point a little too. The real struggle in any endurance race, the thing that makes it absolutely absorbing, is going on inside. Husaby, at his peak, could go for half an hour with his heart rate between 192 and 195 beats per minute, an almost unimaginable strain on body and will. Ray Browning, another ski champion and the winner of several Ironman triathlons, tried to explain: "When things are rolling along easily in a race, you have a broad view—there may be a lot of humor in the pack. As things start to get harder and harder, your attention and focus just close right down, it becomes very singular. It becomes, *what can I do right this second to go fast?*" And *that* is exciting, though in the stoic code of endurance sports it's often hard to read the struggle on the faces of the racers. They don't even like to talk about the pain, for fear of giving in to a kind of weakness. When I brought it up with Husaby, he nodded, but instead of telling me stories he referred me to Luke Bodensteiner's book, *Endless Winter.* Safe in retirement, Bodensteiner was free to tell the truth about how it really felt:

"I was nearing exhaustion at this point," he writes of one race. "My hands were tingling, my balance was going, sweat was running in rivulets down my face, and red juice [he'd spilled from his last water bottle] was frozen solid on to my chest. My brain felt like it was imploding, being squeezed by my rushing, acid-filled flood. And my vision was turning tunnel, fading from light gray to black in the periphery."

If you could somehow manage to make people understand that kind of drama, then surely you'd have legions of interested fans.

Or would you? Is it possible that Husaby was absolutely right, that the Hemingway era has passed, that all the experiences I've been describing in this book are in fact deeply countercultural now?

That night Husaby and I gathered with a couple of dozen other writers and athletes at the Silcox Hut, halfway up Mount Hood. We were there on a junket, to hear the corporate brass of the sporting goods giant Salomon describe all their newest gear, unveil their newest campaigns. Writers were on hand from all the trendiest magazines; they'd spent the day trying out Salomon's newest toys, the latest snowboards and the even-newer Snow-blades, described as inline skates for the snow. The athletes assembled by Salomon included the world extreme skiing champions, truly brave/crazy folk who told tales long into the night of helicoptering to the top of remote peaks and racing down, air-borne as often as not, crashing with ligament-wrecking frequency. They were great athletes, but from a completely different tradition than the Nordic skiers, drawing on other kinds of will and courage. And right now they seem to fit the *Zietgeist* like a Lycra suit.

As we sat drinking microbrews and scarfing down hors d'oeuvres, the Salomon officials showed their new video for the coming year. The theme was "free-riding," and I could almost imagine Husaby gnashing his teeth from across the room. "Free-riding" meant a half hour of gorgeous shots of skiers and board-ers and bladers in midair, backlift against Alps and Rockies, floating through space and time. It meant gravity sucking you straight down the hill. Though Salomon dominates the Nordic ski market, that market is so small in this country that the whole half-hour film had one clip, perhaps three seconds long, of Nordic skiers. They were . . . catching air over a bump in a downhill, something that occupies about one-millionth of an average ski race. No long uphill grinds, so panting, no sweat of any kind. No paying the price. Just . . . free-riding.

I stayed up that night reading *Master of the Mile,* a biography of the great runner Jim Ryun, written by John Lake in 1968. It's a document from a very different age. Young Jim was raised in Kansas, a devout member of the Church of Christ, "where dancing was frowned on, but the church fellowship provided many games and glad times: roller skating once a month at Skateland, bowling at the Rose Bowl every Saturday." There was even church league basketball, but Jim wasn't good at it. "I wish I could play those sports well," he thought wistfully. "But some kids have the talent to do those things and other kids don't. I don't have it, that's all."

Then, of course, he discovered track, and soon his mom was having to warm up his dinner when he came home late from practice. Lake describes the "plain dining room," the "crewcut Dad," the "Mom in her dress," the "big glass of cold milk." And he describes the conversation: " 'James, do you really think you're strong enough for all this running?' his mother asked. 'You looked so terribly weak and tired after that race. And there are nights when you barely touch your dinner any more, dragging in here after all that practice. I'm really very worried.' Her husband was worried too, but he respected the discipline and training required by track. He reassured his wife: 'It's something the boy wants to do very badly, dear. Let him alone and we'll see what happens.'"

What happens, of course, is that he drives himself fiercely and turns into a prodigy of a miler. But not a swell-headed prodigy—even when he's picked for the national squad, he keeps running for the Wichita East High School squad, often entering four or five events to get extra points for his team. When he runs indifferently at one meet, his high school coach says, "'Jim, you slacked off. Just because you have enough ability to get by, you think you can take it easy sometimes. It's a bad habit.'" A few months later, writes Lake, the coach scolded him again: "Pizza burgers had been on the lunch menu in the East High cafeteria, and Jim had gulped down several of the highly seasoned meat patties. That afternoon his stomach had ached so much that he was forced to drop out of a cross-country time trial."

Steering safely clear of exotic ethnic food, Ryun makes the Olympic team as a schoolboy—he has to find someone to take his paper route during the Games. In the words of the *Wichita Eagle* editorial that marked that news: "Jim has found the secret of using a greater amount of his talent in the field of distance running, and that secret is plain hard work. Hopefully his achievement will be a model and symbol for other youngsters who have hidden potential—not necessarily in track, but in many fields of endeavor—and need the spark of energy and the oil of persistence to develop it."

So why are there few Ryuns today—why are the best American times in many distance races slower than they were a decade or two ago? Let's perform a Somewhat Unfair Comparison here and consider the career of one Shaun Palmer, a monarch of extreme sports. In the words of *Outside* magazine, "From the day he burst onto the scene as the foul-mouthed, mop-haired 14-year-old snowboarder that everybody called 'Mini-Shred,' Shaun Palmer, as much as any other athlete, has defined the aggressively delinquent ethos that dominated the early days of alternative sports. Partly, of course, it was his go-for-broke approach to

boarding . . . But much of it was related to his style off the course:
a flamingly rude, crude flamboyance combined with a blatant
devotion to the black arts of partying. Palmer was a true sports
punk, hyperactive, substance-abusing . . . and derisive toward the
dignity of sports in general."

He didn't come from a Church of Christ family; his father
left when he was a few months old, and he was raised largely by
his grandmother, who worked as a witness at Harrah's casino in
Lake Tahoe. Soon he was skateboarding and dealing drugs; by
the time he was fourteen, he was winning snowboard contests.
And what he discovered early on was that the crowds—and
especially the advertisers—liked his swagger. He became famous
for trashing hotel rooms, wearing gold lamé outfits, "defecating
on a former girlfriend's wood-burning stove in a successful
effort to break up her dance party." By the time he'd reached
"adulthood," the combination of athletic success and outrageous behavior had left his famous and rich. In the words of his
agent, "I remember last year, when we were in negotiations with
one bike manufacturer, they were really concerned that he was,
like, going to go out and shit on somebody's car. They really
seemed to be worried, so I said, 'Well, hey, isn't that why you
want him, for that exact image?'"

Palmer's unquestionably a great athlete. In midcareer he
took up downhill mountain biking and soon became a champion at that as well. But both his sports involve riding chairlifts
up the mountain—they are Newtonian in the extreme. You can
pursue them while maintaining what Palmer calls a Budweiser
diet. And you can pursue them while insisting it's not about
hard work at all. If you go to Palmer's Web site (where he wonders if he's "the world's greatest athlete"), you're greeted with

this slice of perfectly distilled millennial attitude: "This is my time capsule. Check it out. Enter the contest or buy some stuff. Whatev. Be cool."

Husaby was famous on the Nordic ski circuit as a hard party-ing fellow; he spent the nineties listening to the same speed metal and wearing the same Oakleys as Palmer. But the difference was, essentially, that he was skiing uphill, and that skiing up a hill, right at this particular moment, doesn't fit our culture quite as well as skiing down it.

It's true that we read lots of books about climbing Everest, but maybe that's *because* our culture has advanced past all that. And maybe that's for the best—now that we have chairlifts why *should* we go through the pain of going uphill? Perhaps it makes more sense to aim solely for the sublime rush of speed. At first glance, and perhaps all subsequent glances too, the hyper-disci-pline of an endurance athlete isn't quite as winsome as Palmer's routine of "clutching a Budweiser in one hand and a Red Bull—a caffeinated soda rumored to be spiked with 'synthetic bull testos-terone'—in the other." Maybe the reason great runners come from Kenya now is that Kenyans haven't had the good fortune to fully advance into the latter days of the consumer society. Maybe hurting is as pointless as wrinkles or baldness or all the other atavistic ills we've managed to banish with new technology. Maybe, as Milan Kundera wrote once, "Speed is the form of ecstasy the technical revolution bestowed on man." Maybe will-power is as antiquated as mule power.

Or maybe, as Husaby mused while we wandered along the Mount Hood trails, "We're crossing the same sort of deal the Romans were crossing at the end of their reign. They had as many slaves as they could use, as much empire as they could control.

But it seemed like they really struggled with their mental and spiritual satisfaction."

Here's how the *New York Times* editorial page greeted news of Jim Ryun's world record in 1966: "A track man's real challenge is to himself. It is the frailty of his own muscles, lungs and heart that he must overcome . . . Few endeavors reduce to a purity of concept the nature of all human achievements as this one does." This was just at the dawn of the celebrity age; thirty years later we may mean something different when we discuss achievement.

But those real challenges still exist, and some people still take them up. The next morning Husaby's fiancée and a gang of their friends from Bend arrived early at the Silcox Hut, intent on summiting Hood. They climbed with a fierce eagerness; I was struggling to keep up, breathing hard. A number of jokes about "free-riding" went up and down the line of hikers, and at one point I asked Husaby—who clearly could have been a world-class athlete in any number of disciplines—if he sometimes wished he'd taken up downhill skiing or streetluging or something more in keeping with the moment. He turned on me almost angrily, as if it was the kind of thought he'd had to keep at bay for years. "No way," he almost shouted. "I love my sport, and I know what my sport's done for me. I'm going to be on top of this mountain by noon." And indeed he was.

# 10

Pursuing summer around the globe is considered entirely sane—the planet's largest industry, tourism, derives most of its revenue from the desire for higher temperatures.

Chasing winter is an odder hobby. In part that's because fewer people enjoy dark, cold, slush, icy roads, and the flu. And in part it's because of the globe's lopsided architecture. No matter where you are, traveling toward the equator will infallibly warm you up. But when it's summer in the Northern Hemisphere, it's a lot like summer in most of the Southern Hemisphere too. The continents of the South don't lie near enough the pole to produce much in the way of winter. So if you want, just for instance, to go cross-country ski racing in August, you can choose between one set of groomed trails in Patagonia, another in New Zealand, and three or four along the narrow range of mountains that rise along Australia's southeast corner.

Which explains why I found myself on the endless flight to

Sydney (those who believe it's a small world have never flown Qantas). I'd been training six months, my year was halfway gone, and I was desperate to rev up my motor and put it to the test. And save for that seventy-five feet on Mount Hood, I had gone since April without snow. Long enough!

The weatherman, in his role as vox populi, decries snow because it makes commuting difficult. As if commuting was the noblest aim of man! Surely, in the secret chambers of his heart, even the weatherman loves a snowstorm. Who could not? The sky darkens, the flakes whirl down—and they pile up! Some portion of the atmosphere comes to rest on the ground, stays there for days and weeks and months, hardening, softening, turning dirty, getting a new coat. Everything else on the planet's surface arrives there through patient, diligent effort—it pushes up from below, victualed by the long supply lines of its roots. Rain falls too, of course, but then it disappears, leaking through the pores of the earth. Snow is an enchantment. It turns the sleek fat: bulbous cars, puffy spruces. It turns the world silent—there is no silence like a windless nighttime snowfall. It mutes color. Nothing changes the world like a snowstorm.

The Eskimos may or may not have fifty-six words for snow, but doubtless they can catalog at least that many varieties—the twenty-below snow that squeaks like Styrofoam underfoot, the many-faceted fresh flakes that glint back the light of the moon, the clumping-moist first snows of fall that peel off the wet ground leaving behind brown boot prints, the bulletproof snow refrozen on a bitter morning, the wind-whipped snow that works its way down your collar. Snowman snow, dispirited late-spring snow with its collage of needles and twigs. Snow in feathery drifts that lets you leap from one ledge to the next down a mountain, snow so ice-crusted you need to grab every tree to make it through the forest. Backcountry skiers dig pits and check snow for stability, looking for the unstable powdered-sugar layers that can trigger an avalanche. Ski waxers, magnifying lenses clutched in mittened hands, can tell a sharp flake ready to grab a waxy bottom from a rounded metamorphosed crystal that won't. Snow turning blue under the full moon, pink and orange at sunset, snow drifting over the kitchen windows and turning the house subterranean, snow blowing horizontal in front of a gale.

To this list you can add Australian snow. From Sydney I flew on to Melbourne, and there rented a car for the two-hour drive to Lake Mountain. The road wound through wineries, and then a forest of towering gum trees, before finally arriving at the town of Marysville. It was shirtsleeve weather, but small huts renting tire chains lined the edge of town. Aussie law requires them of anyone entering snow zones, because neither Aussie cars nor Aussie drivers are geared for winter driving. Up the road I went, passing the occasional roadkill wallaby. The fog kept growing thicker, especially once I passed the snow line. We were barely on the edge of winter; the snow seemed always about to change phases, retreat into vapor.

But no mind. The good people of Melbourne were out in force. Their kids, many of whom had never seen snow before, were sliding a small hill on rented toboggans. The adults, some in long skirts, were walking the trails on skis. Before long, though, I was away from the crowds, and gliding lonely through this mist, which reeked of the eucalyptus trees on either side. It was unlike anything I'd ever seen or smelled. God was sucking on cough drops.

And it got only more surreal. A day later I drove a few hours north to the resort town of Falls Creek on the Bogong High Plain, in the middle of this small Australian range. I was too early for the Bogong Moth Festival, an outgrowth of a millennia-old gathering of aborigines who would collect and eat, well, moths. Most of the holiday-makers on hand when I arrived were there for the downhill skiing, on a mountain that would make the average New England slope seem positively Himalayan. But the cross-country touring rivaled any on earth. That first afternoon I skied the flats for hours, past flocks of brilliant red parrots called crimson rosellas. And the next morning, up early to meet my guide, I headed off on to the high plain proper, and boundary-less expanse of bowls and low peaks marked with a few scattered groves of snow gum tress and not much else. The chill night had frozen the snow crusty and fast—you could skate ski in any direction, like a skateboarder in an empty swimming pool. Before I'd gone a friend had told me, "Imagine Vermont without any forest, just snow-covered rock." And he was right; it was like skiing on the moon.

Goggle-eyed as I was, though, I spent at least as much time looking inward, to discern the effects of all my training on my machinery. Some days it seemed as if it all had worked—I'd push off with my remodeled calves and brand-new triceps and I would really go. Other mornings I puffed just as hard as if I'd never run a mile. I knew I'd have a better gauge soon; I was scheduled to mark the last day of my stay by racing in the Paddy Pallin Classic, a twenty-five-kilometer race on the lower slopes of Australia's highest peak, Mount Kosciusko.

Paddy Pallin was the prototypical Australian outdoorsman. In his autobiography, *Never Truly Lost*, he spins one yarn after another: bushwalks through Tasmanian tiger country, swimming through riparian caves. At the age of fifty he learned to ski, a skill he employed to get himself cheerfully lost all across the Australian alps. "With bushwalkers," he writes, "when we face danger and difficulty, something deep inside us responds to the challenge with a fierce joy; and when the trip is over there is a profound satisfaction, far exceeding the normal enjoyment of a pleasant trip." His namesake race makes sure that spirit survives.

The day before this year's vision, I stopped by the race office, where Pallin's daughter Nancy was typing last-minute entries into the computer. "We do have a history of challenging weather conditions," she said cheerfully. "Those lows come howling off the southern ocean, and they just keep howling right across the country. One year the wind was so strong we had trouble stopping skiers as they came across the finish line. We had to go out and catch them. One year we had perfect snow on the ground, and then the wind below 140 kilometers per hour the night before. If you're from the Northern Hemisphere you really can't understand skiing here—just look at those gum trees, all twisted and tortured. But if you'd ever met the man, Paddy himself, it was always about giving it a go."

And the breed had not died. Everywhere I went in Australia's high country I came across bushwalkers, trekkers, adventurers of one kind or another. Most were men, engaged in lonely, dusty, outback epics. Robin Rishworth, for one, had recently taken up skiing after becoming the first person to bike the Canning Stock Road. "It was 1,800 kilometers on dirt with no towns for twenty-six days and nine-hundred—plus sand dunes," he said happily. "I also cycled across the Simpson Desert in five and a half days, and then I put my bike on the summit of the highest mountain in each of Australia's states and territories, even though I usually had to disassemble it and carry it up in my backpack."

There were a few Lycra-clad racers hanging around the start of the Pallin race—Australia fields an Olympic team, which America usually manages to beat. But many more were wearing wool and carrying daypacks. "Battlers," the Aussies call them, guys who just keep going. I looked at them and thought, There's some guys that I can beat. Not only that, the wind was hardly blowing this day. A slight snow was falling, and I was ready. Eager.

Too eager, as it turned out. The race was three laps around an eight-kilometer loop, and it began with a series of uphills. My legs felt like springs at the start—I was flying up hills, passing almost everyone in my wave, skating across snow that was still frozen hard from the night before, still fast. My heart was hammering up above 160 beats per minute according to the monitor on my wrist, but I paid it no mind. I'd started in the second wave, five minutes behind the elite skiers, and it wasn't long before I was entering thoughts of catching them, or at least trying to remember how many older guys went out in that first group. Maybe I was in the money for my age group! God, I felt invincible.

But halfway around that first lap, on a long flat that wound through the snow gums, a fellow passed *me*. True, he was a young guy—a college kid who should have started up front with the top guns. But I felt the euphoria fade, and I felt my adrenaline start to go too. Ray Browning, the champion triathlete, told me once that "even if I'm out there for eight and a half hours, there's always some mechanism inside me that's saying GOOOOOOOO!" *My* mechanism was broken. It started saying, This hurts, and, You're pretty pathetic, and before long my form had disintegrated as quickly as my mood. I took a fall near the end of the first lap, and the second time around I was just slogging on the uphills—not thinking about form or technique, only about how far to the top of the rise. People were passing me now, and far from rousing me to fight, it was just making me grimmer. Near the end of the race, some wool-clad older guy said, "C'mon, mate, rush this hill," and I tried, but that small rise wobbled my knees; all I could do was push myself with my poles for a minute or two. I finished 1:18, twenty-three minutes behind the winner.

I had plenty of time to think on the flight home, and all the next week when I was too jet-lagged to do much more than token running. I kicked myself again and again. Rob said not to worry much—I'd simply committed the most common of rookie sins, gone out too fast and then died. "Your body wasn't able to deal with the lactate. One byproduct of lactic acid is carbon dioxide, and that's why you started to breathe so hard. It's not so much that you were trying to get more oxygen as that you were trying to get rid of $CO_2$." As the fall wore on, he said, my schedule would call for ever more intervals, short bursts at peak intensity that should teach the muscles to clean out waste.

But I wasn't convinced that my heart and lungs were the heart of the problem. I knew I was making physical progress—a year before I wouldn't have even tried to race hard over a distance like that. It was my head that worried me, my will. Pete Vordenberg, a former American Olympian, once described the start of a big race: "I know the pace will slacken eventually and I will be able to recover some, but until then I can look forward to an extreme case of burning legs and straining lungs. There is no conscious decision, no free will. Years of training and racing creates a habit of enduring and hanging on to the skier in front of me regardless of effort . . . *this is the trick, eliminate the brain from all deci-sion-making.* All messages from the body tell the brain that all is not well, and the brain says stop immediately, but the brain is wrong . . . Behind me brains are at work. I can tell this because the bodies they control fall behind." That was mine. At the first sign of adversity my intensity had dropped, my focus dissolved. I was still a normal person—*when it hurt I stopped*. I still had some work to do.

Early in September, Rob and his equally fit fiancée, Carol, were married. They rented out a tennis camp in far northern Vermont for three days and invited friends up for a blowout. Which in this case meant all the miles you could bike, all the hills you could climb, all the lakes you could paddle. Every car in the parking lot had a rack on the top; it was like a Mafia wedding, except instead of pinky rings everyone wore spandex. A huge bowl of party favors sat by the entrance: Clif bars in every flavor of the carbohydrate rainbow. Great endurance athletes kept wandering in to eat some more before the next trail run—there's Murray Banks, king of masters-level cross-country skiing, and there's his son Jeff, a Middlebury College star and Olympic hopeful, just back from the glaciers of Norway. And there's Ray Browning, winner of seven Ironman triathlons. Colleen Cannon, who read Mary Oliver's poem "Wild Geese" during the ceremony, was the former world champion pro triathlete. At dinner, Sue and I sat next to Jim Miller, who was still running the same 2:20 marathon pace that he'd managed in the 1980 Olympic trials—Jim explained that he had subsisted for many years on "Miller Compound," a base of brown rice and lentils to which he added herbs, tuna, peanut butter, low-fat cottage cheese, and raisins. "If it was getting too dry after a few days, I'd douse it in V-8 juice," he said cheerfully.

I didn't exactly fit in (these people were not just fit, they were fast), but I now felt as if I understood a little of what they'd each gone through. I was in the middle of the very hardest weeks of the training year, eighteen or nineteen hours of running and roller-skiing. Eighteen or nineteen hours may not sound like *that* much—only half a work-week—but it meant running twenty miles one day, and uphill intervals the next day, and twenty miles again the day after that. My elbow twinged a little, probably from pounding my poles into the pavement as I roller-skied, and I had to eat five meals a day to keep 160 pounds on my six-foot-three frame. My body fat fell so low that I'd start shivering after five minutes in a swimming pool, but I felt strong: I'd look at my schedule and see that it called for just two hours of running and I'd think, An easy day. I was getting there.

The longest day of my entire year came on a Saturday morning, September 19, a week after Rob's wedding. My parents were visiting, and they took Sophie off for a morning of fun. I was supposed to keep my heart rate in zone 1 for 3 hours and 55 minutes, so I roller-skied fifteen miles and then started running the hills west of town. By the time I finished I was moving pretty slowly but feeling pretty exhilarated. It's all downhill from here, I was telling myself as I crested the top of the final hill. I'll never have to go that far again. Yes!

My mother was waiting for me when I finished the run. My dad was a hundred yards away, walking back and forth, and he looked a little odd. He was *lurching* a bit. "He's testing himself," Mom said, with a frantic edge in her voice. And slowly the story started to come out. In August he'd been hiking hard in the Cascades of his native Washington, feeling fine. But when he got home he'd begun stumbling a bit—once he fell right over. And, Mom added, some days he slurred his words. Dad had been chalking it up to the late-summer humidity, or perhaps a sinus infection, and he'd been trying to rally (and reassure) himself by walking faster, working up a sweat. But when I took him aside that afternoon he confessed that his right side felt weak. Could he have had a small stroke? he asked me. As soon as he said it, I felt myself starting to panic—he'd never been seriously ill in his whole life; it had never even entered my mind that at sixty-eight he'd start to decline. But as soon as he said the word, I knew it must be true; it would explain the balance, the speech, even the mild displays of completely uncharacteristic temper.

And so he promised to visit the neurologist the minute he got home to Boston. I bid them goodbye with a sour taste in the back of my throat and watched him wheel out of the driveway for the four-hour drive home. The next day he phoned to say thanks for sending him to the doctor, who was convinced that indeed he'd had a very mild stroke—a stroke whose effect would likely disappear over time. He'd scheduled an MRI for later in the week just to make sure there was nothing more, but he told Mom and Dad to go ahead planning a trip to Mexico; I could tell from his voice that Dad was immensely relieved just to have a diagnosis.

And I was too. I spent a little time thinking about the Meaning of It All—how your body would eventually betray you no matter how fit you got—and then I went back to work, because racing season was coming into distant view. The weather began to change; a front came through one night, dropping temperatures down in the low 30s, threatening the tomatoes. And the weatherman actually talked about "the possibility of sleet or snow on the high ridges." The S word hadn't been heard in these parts since early May, and it made me quiver inside just like always. I knew, rationally, that skiable snow was at least two months away, and yet I knew, too, that I'd listen closely to the weather forecast every single morning.

I started stacking firewood in earnest that week, and while I was working Friday afternoon I looked up to see our dog, Barley, trotting toward me with something in her mouth. At first I thought it was a shoe, but when she dropped it for me I saw it was a hawk—dead, but utterly unmarked, a broadwing, all strength and sinew. I called Sophie out, and we spread its strong gray feathers, examined its powerful beak and talons, and then wrapped it in plastic and put it in the freezer so that she could take it to school the next week. For a few minutes we speculated on how it might have died, and then I went back to the woodpile.

When I looked up a few minutes later, Sue was standing there in the fading light with tears running down her cheeks. My mom had just called. The MRI showed that Dad had a brain tumor, "an aggressive nonbenign tumor." They were operating on Tuesday. Just like that.

I hugged her for a long time, and then headed straight out into the woods, cursing and crying and carrying on. The only rational thought I can remember is, How do people without forests ever handle tragedy? How do they convince themselves there's some kind of purpose and order and cycle to life? Mostly I just cried. And kept crying that evening as I tried to talk on the phone. Mom said the doctor had told them that even with the operation "the long-term average survival" was twelve months, which put a new spin on the whole idea of long-term. For me, twelve months was a "training cycle." I was still sobbing when Dad came on the phone. "This is ridiculous, isn't it?" he said with a rueful chuckle. He'd been shaving when I called, and for some reason that made me even sadder. How do you manage to look in the mirror when someone has just told you that in a year you won't be there?

A couple of weeks before, I'd visited some actuarial Web site that let you calculate your likely life span. Didn't smoke; long-lived relatives; plenty of exercise; low cholesterol—when I tapped the final button it told me I was going to die at ninety-three. I'm certain that Dad would have gotten the same result. *His* dad had lived to ninety-five; he had three considerably older siblings, and they were all still strong and well. He was strong and active—he'd retired from the newspaper the year before, only to write his first book, which had been published in the spring to good reviews. Another quarter century seemed a completely reasonable bet. But there was no little button on the actuarial table to calculate the random appearance of something called glioblastoma, the most virulent form of brain cancer.

When we got to Boston the next day, the change was obvious. Six days earlier his speech had been a little slurred and his gait had lurched from time to time. Three days earlier he was still strong enough to drive to church and chair a meeting. Today, Saturday, his triumph had been walking the twenty yards to the Adirondack chairs in the backyard. That was now the outer limit of his world. He told us about finding out the bad news: The surgeon had pronounced his death sentence, and then said he should choose. "I could get a big bottle of Scotch and have a wonderful last night before going into a coma, or I could have this surgery and that would keep me going a little longer." It was a choice we would all mull over many times in the months to come.

At 3 a.m. that morning I woke from a dead sleep to the sound of a crash from the room above, and I knew instantly what it was. My brother, Tom, and I arrived at the same moment, to find Dad sprawled out across the bedroom floor—he'd gotten up to go to the bathroom and pitched right over. We finally got him to the toilet, closed the door, and he toppled again; now his world could no longer include privacy.

By 4:45, the nurse from the surgical team that would operate on Tuesday was on hand. She told us the swelling in his brain must be growing fast, and she started feeding him steroids and anti-seizure drugs. Her goal was to let him stay at home for the thirty-six hours till the operation, so she taught my brother and me how to walk him along the hall, how to hold him while he peed. We were groggy, disbelieving, sad beyond words. And yet it was a magical day in some words. Sophie and her cousin Ellie, not quite one, spent the day playing on his bed. Ellie dismantled the funny pages; Sophie went outside to gather a jar of acorns as a present. Mostly we talked and talked and talked, stories of old times and good times. Sports memories in particular kept coming back—they provide stable markers against the power of time to erode impression. He talked about his boyhood love, the Seattle Rainiers of the Pacific Coast League, about sitting on "Tightwad Hill" behind the stadium when he lacked cash for a ticket. I remembered the day when I was small and he made me stand in front of the TV set to watch Carl Yastrzemski bat in his Triple Crown season. We all listened to the radio as Mark McGwire hit number 69 and then number 70.

Somehow Dad made the hard parts—going in the shower with him, say—okay. In late afternoon Sophie appeared with a batch of temporary tattoos, and we spent an hour decorating each other—giant, detailed bugs crawling across heads and arms. And if we all lost it when she had us sing "Amazing Grace" as our blessing before dinner, we knit it back together as the evening went on. It was hopelessly joyous.

As I was taking off his slippers to put him to bed, I could see the hard, veiny calves that only a month ago were powering him up high mountains in his native Northwest. They were useless now. Was he useless? What did it mean to lose your body in a week? And what would it mean, twenty-four hours hence, to lose some large chunk of your mind?

The next morning we got him downstairs, one step at a time. Like a schoolkid on the final day of summer vacation, I was obsessed with the idea of the *last*—was this his last time upstairs in his bedroom, his last time walking outside? We drove in to the hospital, and though he was in the passenger seat he was still fully *competent*—giving directions to the hospital, figuring out the best side streets to take around the traffic. Once in the door, though, he passed into another, yet-smaller world, where his abilities meant nothing. The first person to talk to him was a Hispanic admitting nurse who spoke almost no English; she just handed him a bottle and kept saying, "Make peepee in cup." When they finally gave him a room, we just sat around the bed, getting gloomier by the minute. The surgeon finally came for his pre-op visit, and Dad asked one question: "Will my personality change?"

"I hope not," the doctor said.

We watched the next morning as they wheeled him out of his room to the operating theater, and then we went downstairs for the long wait. After an hour I couldn't stand it and, beeper in my pocket, went to the local gym for ninety minutes of explosive, angry lifting. It was after lunch before the doctor appeared to give us the news. Dad had come through surgery okay, but the pathology was exactly what he suspected: glioblastoma, grade 4. The worst grade. He couldn't get it all, it had already spread to both lobes. Sorry. "Sometimes we open someone up and look at a tumor and say, 'There's just not much we can do for that one.' His is one of those. If I'd tried to cut out any more of it, I would have been taking too much brain—you wouldn't have liked what I'd given back to you." The next few months, the doctor said, would be "the good time," a phrase that would come to haunt us. He'd cut away enough tumor that the swelling should drop until the tumor regrew. When it did, the "good time" would be paid for with a tough time; he would slide into a coma, contract pulmonary disease, and die.

When the surgeon left, we collapsed on top of each other and we sobbed. But when they finally let us up to see him, Dad looked—beautiful. A turban of bandages wrapped his head, but beneath it his face was eerily young, as if he was in his twenties. The sparkle was back in his eyes. It didn't hurt that when we turned on the TV the Red Sox were leading the Indians in game one of their playoff series behind seven RBIs from Mo Vaughn. Dad was making jokes—he whose head had been sawed open and then the two halves pulled apart by traction a few hours before.

This much was clear: His personality had *not* changed, not one whit. Doubtless it would darken when the tumor recurred, when the swelling built up again. The hope, though, was that we'd bought ourselves a few months to deal with it, a window of time to make peace with his passing. Nothing more—no real hope for miracles.

But even that respite, we soon learned, might be asking a lot. The post-operative clarity faded over the next few days; probably surgical swelling, the doctor said, the result of the scalpel and not the tumor. Certainly it would fade, and we'd have our "good time." For now, nurses kept appearing to perform neurological tests. Dad would try desperately to touch his right hand to his nose, but he couldn't quite figure out where his nose resided; he looked spooked, depressed. He'd try to move his legs and fail. It took him seventy-two hours to get out of the neurological intensive care unit, not the twenty-four they'd predicted. I left for a day, and when I phoned back the "good news" was that he'd moved his bowels. It dawned on me that his best day in this new world would have been the worst day of any other week of his life.

And so we settled into the pattern of small victories and somewhat larger defeats that must mark most terminal illness. There were constant decisions to make: Should he undergo a six-week course of radiation therapy, which on the one hand might prolong the "good time" by keeping the tumor temporarily at bay, and which on the other hand would exhaust him? We settled on yes, mostly because that's what the doctor was urging. "In for a dime, in for a dollar" pretty much defined our strategy. And so they shifted Dad to a "rehabilitation hospital" in the suburbs where, after daily morning trips by ambulance to the radiation ward, he would return for afternoons of physical therapy.

The therapy rooms reminded me of the world where I'd spent much of the last year—they were filled with weight machines, parallel bars, treadmills. But here, in place of the ersatz philosophy of the gym, real struggle prevailed. People groaned not with the effort of inflating their deltoids, but with the effort of walking four steps on an artificial leg. Dad's workouts, as tightly scheduled and as exhausting as mine, involved batting a balloon back and forth with the therapist, folding washcloths, unscrewing a jar top, kicking a ball. He could swing his right foot perhaps an inch, enough to nudge the ball along the floor, but no more. When he tried to steer his wheelchair, it inevitably drifted to the right till he hit a wall, reflecting the now-distorted architecture of his brain. His major triumph: learning to apply and disengage the wheelchair brake.

Through it all I kept running. I suppose I should have stopped, if only because it seemed in such poor taste, calibrating my body's improvement as Dad's withered away. But there was nothing else to structure my life. No one expected me at an office. I was commuting between my adult and boyhood homes (in fact, I was sleeping on the bed I'd slept on as a boy, which happened to be the same bed Dad had slept on in his youth). There was no way I could write—when I tried to still my mind enough to string two thoughts together, I invariably began to weep. Motion seemed to relax me; I'd put on my headphone and run straight through *All Things Considered*, occupying at least the foreground of my mind.

Anyway, Dad had been more interested than anyone else in my project. He'd told me stories about running the beaches of Puget Sound in his hiking boots to prep for baseball season. When I'd gotten my heart monitor, he tried it on right away. Now he

was hooked to a heart rate monitor more often than I was. I'd
spent the year thinking about endurance. Now I was going to
learn something about it for real.

Since I was staying these weeks in the home I'd grown up in, I was
running through a scrapbook of my early life. Each morning my
route took me through the playground of my elementary school:
Here's the spot where we used to run the fifty-yard dash in gym,
the place where I first learned I was slow. Here's the junior high
soccer field, where I started my career as a sportswriter; here's the
wing of the high school where I spent a happy senior year surrounded by the paraphernalia of a debater—note cards, flow-
charts, cases full of trophies. It constantly amazed me to see how
*small* my native suburb really was: The center of town, with its
stores and restaurants, was a ten minutes' run from home, not the
car-required voyage I remembered from my childhood. I got up
one morning to run intervals on the giant hill at the end of the
block, my downfall as a beginning bike rider, only to discover
that it took forty-five seconds to sprint up the small rise, hardly
enough to raise my heart rate.

That same Alice-on-her-first-pill sensation of being too big
stayed with me when I was around Dad. If he had declined slowly,
over the years, then I might have gradually gotten used to the idea
that I was now more dependable, more stable, more planted in the
world than he. But the switch had happened over the space of a
weekend. I couldn't shake my confusion. Sometimes I was as
groggy as he was. I remember watching one night when a neurological nurse quizzed him about the day, the month, the name of
the president. He couldn't quite guess any of them, though he

knew the White House belonged to an Irishman: "Kelly?" "O'Callahan?" If she'd turned and asked me who *I* was, I'm not sure I could have answered any better. Was I a young thirty-seven, allowed to think of myself as barely a grownup because there was still a cutting edge of real adults out ahead of me in the world? Or had I been launched into some other role the first time I held my father while he peed?

I'd begun this compulsive exercising on the premise that I was at the tail end of my youth. Now it was all too easy to calculate that if I lived as my father was going to, I was already halfway used up. But I could feel the second half of my life starting in more complicated ways too. Identities long-fixed shifted back and forth. Sometimes, more than in many years of living at a distance, I was still his son. The NBA was on strike that fall, so the TV would replay classic games of the past. I remember one night sitting by his bed to watch the great Celtics team of the eighties take on Michael Jordan's first playoff squad. We'd watched those Celtics a thousand times; for years, on my birthday, he would take me out to eat downtown, and then we'd walk the cold streets beneath the Green Line to the old Boston Garden to watch that McHale-Bird-Parish frontcourt work its magic. And here they were again, hair now unfashionably shaggy, just barely beating the emergent Jordan. Dad would watch, and sigh in appreciation at a great pass from Bird, a towering McHale rebound. For an hour, life was in its normal track.

With Mom, memory could take him back much further. One night in his hospital room, after an especially impossible day when a blood clot had demanded yet another surgery to install a filter in his vein, she started reading him passages from David Remnick's new biography of Muhammad Ali. Or Cassius Clay, as he was known when my dad had interviewed him before the Archie Moore fight an impossibly long time ago. But maybe nothing in one's own life history ever seems too far distant: Dad told stories till he fell asleep that night about the sleek young fighter.

But then the next morning would dawn, and we'd need yet again to make some impossible decision: more radiation, say. Dad would doze off while the doctor was explaining the options, and we'd be left trying to figure out what he might want, what we might want. Momentum usually won out; ever since he'd decided on surgery instead of a bottle of Scotch, each next step seemed to follow semi-logically from the one before. Having scraped the tumor from his mind, it seemed senseless not to try to hold it at bay a little while with radiation. As the weeks wore on, though, it became clear that he was not going to recover significant strength or coordination; the brain is a mysterious, unpredictable organ, and who knew exactly what the scalpel had excised? In any event, he was making less progress than they had predicted, and the goal of all the physical therapy diminished. Instead of teaching him to regain real function in his muscles, the single aim became training him to help in the process of transferring himself from bed to wheelchair, and vice versa. If he learned that, he could go home and Mom could take care of him by herself when no one else was around. The technique, as detailed and precise as a good skiing kick, involved lifting his butt an inch up off the bed, and then sliding himself in two stages about a foot and a half into the wheelchair. He would push himself up on his knuckles, slide ten inches, rest thirty seconds till the panting subsided, then make the next assault. Each time he'd forget the sequence and need to be reminded; each time it left him red-faced and tired.

Progress was ephemeral. All this training, and for what? It

wasn't like my training. I may have bonked when it came time to race in Australia, but I knew I was getting steadily stronger and fitter. Not Dad. He worked all afternoon stretching his rubber bands, lifting his tiny dumbbells, and yet his body decayed faster than he could build it up. I came in to the rehab center one morning and found him in an uncharacteristic rage. Some doctor had wandered through that morning (one of the glories of managed care was that unknown doctors constantly drifted in and out of our lives) and remarked to him, on the basis of a handshake, that he was getting weaker. Dad was outraged, agitated. He didn't want to go to therapy that afternoon, but I talked him into it. You followed your schedule no matter what; sometimes that seemed about all my year had taught me.

# 12

If I needed a metaphor for my autumn, it came in early November. I was back in the Adirondacks for a week, and I'd noticed some fresh new pavement on a back road on the far side of the Hudson River. Fresh pavement, to a roller skier, exerts a nearly gravitational pull. It isn't snow, but it's the next best thing—smooth and fast, free from the constant rattle of worn macadam. What I hadn't noticed was just how steep the hills were on this particular road. I was, as always, wearing a bike helmet, but I'd forgotten my kneepads. Should I go anyway? I'd driven all the way over, and the light was already fading, and so, predictably, I went for it. For an hour I skied the hills, tucking for fast descents, powering up with short, choppy kicks, feeling pretty damn strong. And then, predictably, a dog ran out at the bottom of a hill just as a car passed on my left—I was down in a second, with both knees scraped open. Predictably, I jumped up, in the way that guys do when they've fallen, as if to say, Oh, I meant to do that. I waved off the stricken driver—and as soon as he was out of sight I sat right back down to consider. True, my knees were bleeding dramatically, soaking my shredded tights, but on the other hand I had ninety minutes left to go to finish my workout. I'd snapped a pole when I fell, so I clearly wasn't going to keep skiing, but I had my sneakers in the car. And so—predictably?—I went for a run, telling myself that as long as I kept bleeding my knees wouldn't get infected, that bending them at every step would prevent me from stiffening up. All of which was clearly stupid, so it is at least possible that I just wanted to hurt, and to keep going through the hurt.

Though I turned the bathwater bright red when I finally got home, I escaped without structural damage—just enormous scabs that cracked open for months whenever I bent my knees, weeping just enough blood to weld to whatever pants I was wearing. I made do with the NordicTrack for a few days, but soon enough I was out and about—just in time to return to Lake Placid and the great treadmill for the final readout on my year's training. A light snow was actually falling as I drove north, coating the tops of the highest peaks; I could watch the fat flakes starting to collect on the ground outside the Olympic Training Center as I warmed up on the treadmill. Before long, though, my vision had narrowed down to the blinking heart rate monitor in front of me, and to Ken Rundell and Rob, who stood, arms crossed, near the speed controls, watching me go.

The first part of the test seemed easy enough—I was running fluidly for the fifteen minutes it took to prick my fingers and analyze my blood chemistry. I even overheard Ken telling Rob that my "lactate profile" had improved considerably. But then the treadmill speeded up, and my mouth turned dry around the rubber bit that trapped my exhalations, and my resolve started to slip. I lasted longer than I had in the spring, but only because of my new body—as the test reached the gut check stage, mine seemed to be missing. I pushed my heart rate up to 175 beats per minute, racing the ever-steeper treadmill, but in the spring I'd managed 180. This time I couldn't keep myself going. It hurt, that's why. The instant I heard Ken say, "Can you give me another thirty seconds?" I knew that was exactly what I'd give him. But I also knew that even on that tilting, speeding belt there was a minute more left inside of me that I hadn't been able to reach down and extract.

The same thing happened an hour later when I repeated the text while double-poling on roller skis. Murray Banks, the masters champion I'd met at Rob's wedding, had been in for testing the week before. "He lasted seven minutes before he crapped out," said Rundell. "Let's see you beat him," he added, not once but several times. Needless to say, I didn't—as soon as I'd eclipsed my two-minute debacle of the previous spring, I began thinking about the end. "Maybe you can hit four," said Ken—and that's precisely what I did, my mind shutting down my body before it began to hurt too much. I had remained safely in my comfort zone. "Double-poling is the key to ski racing," Ken said sternly, "and yours is still a nightmare." Only in the body fat department did I score a convincing triumph—according to the calipers, eight months of dry bagels and skim milk had dropped me from 12 percent body fat to 6.69 percent, right on the upper edge of the range for elite male endurance athletes.

Once I'd showered, once all the computers had finished bar-graphing my results, Rob and I sat down with the printouts to figure out just who I had become. My VO2 Max, key measure of my ability to turn the air around me into speed and power, had gone from 54 milliliters of oxygen per minute per kilogram of body weight to 58—a jump of about 7 percent, right in line with Rob's prediction. My anaerobic threshold, as expected, remained at about 166 heartbeats per minute—go any faster and I would soon blow up. The rate at which lactic acid built up in my muscles had fallen sharply—all those miles had built the plumbing network necessary to flush it away. Bottom line: Running at my anaerobic threshold, my velocity had increased half a mile per hour. If I spent an hour running at my highest sustainable pace, I'd go half a mile farther than I would have eight months before. Twice around a high school track.

Rob, of course, professed delight, beaming at me as we ate our vegetable soup afterwards. "You've had a 45 percent improvement in body fat, your lactate threshold is 25 percent better—your engine is burning hotter at a lower lactate production. It means you can ski at a faster pace longer."

So we talked on about what physiology dictated in terms of strategy for the approaching races. "On the shorter races, you can stay right at your threshold heart rate, up in the 160s," he said. "For a longer race, you need to dial it back about ten beats. If you go too hard on the first few hills, that lactic acid accumulates in your muscles, and eventually it will slow you down, just like it did in Australia. You want negative splits—you want to ski the second half of the race faster than the first." Remember, remember, remember: "It's a game of figuring out how far back from the finish line you can stop being cautious. If you go for it too early, you risk blowing up—but you also risk surprising yourself."

My main task now, he insisted, was staying healthy—no more roller-skiing—and focusing on speed and technique while I gradually reduced the high-mileage workouts that had dominated summer. "You've done the basework. Look at it this way, for months, you've been cutting out a tabletop, sanding it with the rough grit. Now there's just the fine stuff left to do."

And part of me *did* feel exhilarated. It had worked the way it was supposed to, all those hours and miles. Mine was not the physique of a champion, but that had never been in the cards; what I had done was maximize my genetic potential, grown about as powerful as my ancestry would allow.

But the day left me feeling unsettled too. If I'd managed to make physical progress, I wasn't at all sure I'd grown stronger mentally, emotionally. Those last few minutes of the treadmill test worried me. When things had gotten really tough, I had looked for a way out, quit early, done enough to maintain my honor in the eyes of onlookers. But no more. My heart might have become more efficient, but my *heart* seemed no stronger. The flesh was willing and even able, but the spirit was weak. If my endurance had improved as measured in milliliters of oxygen per kilogram of body weight, my endurance as measured in more subtle ways seemed hardly to have budged.

Truth be told, I was beginning to question whether endurance was such a grand goal anyhow.

From the moment I'd learned of Dad's first conversation with the surgeon—the Scotch or scalpel talk—part of me had been wondering whether we should be keeping him alive or not. He hadn't progressed even as fast as the doctor's grim forecast; at every meeting we'd press the specialists with questions about whether his condition would improve, and all we'd get was the Ph.D. equivalent of shrugs. Maybe the radiation would reduce the size of the tumor enough that he'd have a temporary respite, enough that the "good time" would finally arrive. Maybe not.

In the meantime, he was home, and the burden on Mom was crushing. Tom and I tried to be there much of the time, but we each had a family and responsibilities, so like most adult children in this far-flung world, we spent a lot of time feeling guilty and talking on the phone, trying to help with arrangements. The HMO professed to believe that a couple of hours of nursing assistance a day was all Mom needed; never mind that Dad outweighed her by eighty or ninety pounds. She hired extra aides to come in the evening and help her get him out of bed; the next-door neighbor's son slept upstairs now just in case he rolled out of bed and she couldn't get him back in. New pills piled up almost daily; dosages changed with every visit to the doctor; Mom was awake by six to give him his first medications of the day, and still up at midnight to feed him the final batch. At first they were to share a bed, but within a night or two it was clear he required a special hospital model, so she slept nearby on the couch. When I thought about the burden she was under, I doubted I could handle anything like it. And she didn't have her partner of forty years to talk it over with, the way she'd talked over every other crisis of their marriage. There was no way to tell Dad how hard it all had become; just the opposite, in fact. "I pictured him coming home, and us having time to read, to sit and talk together, but it's not like that," she told me one day. And yet she kept going forward, forward, forward, like—well, like an elite athlete. In her case, though, it wasn't uphill intervals and mental imagery that had laid the base. It was year upon year of loving, so consistently that the giving had become instinctive.

Dad had his own battles. Glioblastoma came with one sweet mercy; like most brain cancers, it created little direct pain. At the same time, it robbed him of clarity, clouded his memory. From the day of the operation, we were rarely sure exactly what he knew. One day, at a meeting with the radiation oncologist, the doctor tried to explain how the procedure would work—the marks they'd ink on his skull, the six weeks of daily treatment, the hope they could shrink the tumor enough that he'd have a few more months. He nodded his head sleepily all through the talk, and then said: "So you mean this might come back in five years?" You could argue his confusion was a blessing, but it didn't seem that way to me. He'd always been a realist, and he would want to know he was dying. If this "good time" wasn't going to allow him to prepare for his death, then what use was it?

And so we continued on in a sort of limbo, never sure what we were preparing for—or what we were hoping for. There were good *moments,* to be sure, enough of them to confuse us at the very least. Friends and family arrived from around the country and usually he could rouse himself for their visits. Dear neighbors, whose son was a construction engineer, took just a weekend to build a wheelchair ramp worthy of the Trump Tower off the back of the deck. We wondered if he'd ever get to use it—but one day Tom pushed him up the ramp as fast as he could go, and Dad laughed and laughed. Always, his granddaughters, easier than the rest of us with his facility, could draw him out. On Halloween, he rolled the halls of the rehab hospital in Sophie's witch hat, grinning happily. "I cannot believe how close I feel to my family," he said, over and over. We tried to have a family dinner whenever possible, and some nights it worked wonderfully—Dad at the head of the table, watching all the talk with great pleasure, sometimes throwing in a small joke. Once some visiting child messed up and called him George instead of Gordon. "I'm curious, but I'm not *that* curious," he said. Other nights, and no one could predict when, he'd be slumped so far over in his wheelchair that he'd almost topple—we'd take turns standing behind him and trying to hold him upright long enough to eat. If he got too tired, then getting him back in bed was nearly impossible.

So there were times—when a blood clot in his leg required the operation to install a filter in his vein, for instance—when I half hoped he'd simply die. Or more than half. I told myself it was because his quality of life was so diminished, reduced with stunning suddenness to painful, pointless exercises with twenty-year-old physical therapy students. I told myself it was because I feared Mom would wilt under the strain. But I knew I wanted it over, too.

Some days it was simply too hard to deal with the idea that Dad was dependent on us—that is to say, that we couldn't depend on him. Perhaps it's easier if this process takes place in slow motion, if there's a slow exchange of leadership, of responsibility; perhaps it's harder. I don't know. All I know is how existentially disturbing it was to have to clear out the tubes on a clogged catheter for the man who, three months earlier, had been the single most unchanging and uncomplicated person in my life. That sounds callow, and it is.

A year or so before Dad had gotten sick, *Salon* magazine had asked me to review M. Scott Peck's new book about euthanasia, *Denial of the Soul.* Its powerful argument convinced me that Dr. Jack Kevorkian was not as correct as I'd always assumed. That is to say, there are good reasons for sticking it out until the end, especially if you aren't in hopeless pain. Peck claims that dying is one of the best (and last) chances for self-education—in particular, for learning how to deny the ego, to engage in the process of "the self emptying itself of the self." In the last months and weeks of a life, he writes, one might learn "how to negotiate a middle path between control and total passivity, how to welcome the responsible care of strangers, how to be dependent once again. How to trust; maybe even, out of existential suffering, how to pray or talk with God."

The first time I read it, I found it lovely, convincing. And I still did. It makes a case for—well, it makes a case for endurance. And a better case than any of the faux philosophizing of the fitness magazines, with their endless consumer concentration on self-esteem, self-empowerment. If we pay attention to the mystics, there probably aren't "10 Ways to a Happier Life." There's probably only one, and it has to do with reining in the ego.

But I knew that for my dad, who really *was* a great man, that victory had been won decades before; he worked as purely from unselfish love as my mom did. In the four decades I'd known them, I'd never heard them argue; each instinctively anticipated the needs of the other. One morning, unsure if he was focused or not, Mom came into Dad's sickroom with some piece of news, and said, "Guess what?" Before she could continue he said, "About this love affair we're having?" It was that kind of marriage.

As for me, if watching someone die can perform the same kind of ego-curling magic Peck recommends, I wasn't sure I was ready for it. Endurance hurt, I knew that. When the treadmill got steep enough, I started looking around for someone to turn it off.

Whenever we were with the doctors, no matter how much of a fog he seemed to be in, Dad would ask that they treat his cancer "aggressively." But one night, when I was talking to him very late, he said, "If it's going to be like this all the time, then there has to be a cutoff somewhere." Amen, I thought. Where's the guy with the switch?

# 13

All summer long the town of West Yellowstone in Montana caters to the Winnebago tribe, wheeling through on their way into the park; all winter long, until recent rule changes, snowmobilers ruled the town, their two-stroke engines giving it the nastiest air in the nation—the rangers manning the park entrance booth wore masks to guard their lungs. But for one week in late November, West Yellowstone is a republic of the fit.

For three decades, the nation's best and most rabid Nordic ski racers have gathered in West Yellowstone for Thanksgiving week. They come for a week of early-season training on the most reliable snow in the lower 48: Even if the groomed trails on the edge of town are still bare, there's always skiing on the high ridges that ring the valley. They come for a master's camp, with some of the finest instructors on the continent. And they come to be in a place where, for once, everyone else understands this particular obsession. That is to say, every motel has waxing benches spread out somewhere in the lobby (and signs warning of the dire consequences if you dare uncork the nasty stuff in your room). Every buffet features carafes of skim milk—if you want whole, you have to ask. And everybody you see—*everybody*—is thin to gaunt. It's like a convention of stick figures.

When Dad got sick, I canceled my trip. But as it turned out, it was easier for all concerned to postpone the Final Thanksgiving a few days, so at the last second I decided to go after all—to push every discussion of radiation and responsibility out of my head for a few days. I was spending the week with the Factory Team, America's best pro squad. "Pro" is used very loosely here—their total budge would pay for about half a second-string safety in the NFL. But the Factory Team, sponsored by Salomon Boots, Fischer Skis, Swix Wax, and a lot of smaller companies, managed to pay small stipends to many of the great American skiers of the nineties: Carl Swenson, who had broken through in some big European races; Laura McCabe, Pete Vordenberg, and Laura Wilson, each twice an Olympian; Nathan Schultz, who had starred for Colorado in the NCAAs. There were old-timers like Erich Wilbrecht, who had raced in the biathlon as long ago as the Albertville Olympics in 1992—and there were newcomers, like David Chamberlain, a college all-American the year before in New Hampshire. And there was my friend from Oregon, Ben Husaby, who was winding down his career with a year or two on the Factory Team squad. They'd all been gathered together by Andrew Gerlach, who described himself as a "recovering athlete"—when his racing career ended, he'd founded a company called Endurance Enterprises, and persuaded Fischer and Salomon to fund the Factory Team. Members of the squad raced in most of the country's big races wearing their garish billboard suits; they ran clinics the day before at ski shops; when they won they made sure they held their skis logo-side-up for whatever cameras were in the area—in short, they provided what exposure they could for a chronically underexposed sport.

Gerlach was there to greet me when I arrived late in the afternoon on a Thursday, skidding over the pass from Idaho Falls in a light snowfall. "Want to go for a ski?" he asked, and I did, and so laced on my new pair of Salomon Pilot boots and my new pair of Fischer skate skis (did I mention that these were made by Salomon and Fischer, respectively, and are in my opinion highly *excellent*?). The trails at West Yellowstone were a three-minute walk from the Holiday Inn, and the sidewalk was crowded with Lycra-clad racers commuting to and from workouts, walking at the quick clip of athletes. We reached the start of the ski tracks and clicked in to our bindings; Gerlach may have retired from his racing career, but it took me about a hundred yards to realize I was going to have to struggle to keep up. My heart rate was soaring on the hills, and I felt as if I had no form at all as I watched him slither up the steepest inclines. But at least I was back on snow. Andrew went back to the hotel after half an hour—he had a thousand chores to do all week—but I kept going for another couple of hours in the gathering twilight, slowly touring the network of lovely trails with lovelier views, out over the wide expanses of Yellowstone territory. After all the endless running, the frictionless, bounceless feel of ski on snow was elegant, sexy. Even the sweat that chilled on my brow during the downhills felt good.

And so for a couple of days my life fell into the pattern of a real ski racer at a real training camp. A long ski in the morning, a long lunch, another long ski in the afternoon: mileage, volume, all at an easy pace. Temperatures hovered near freezing, warm for

West Yellowstone in November, but the ski tracks stayed firm. The town was filling, not just with ski racers from around the country, but with the representatives of the small industry that serves them: the wax companies, the guys who make hydration backpacks, the folks with the lightest, most high-tech ski poles. One night early in the week, most of the members of the Factory Team assembled for what they called Christmas, the distribution of all the gear from their sponsors. They already had their skis and boots—they'd been shipped this year's models weeks before so that they could get to work preparing them in their own particular ways. But now all the lesser angels were spreading their gear around, a free-for-all of underwear and fleece, energy bars and sunglasses. And I was stricken, suddenly, with a green-eyed lust I've rarely known.

How unexpected a feeling! I've spent much of my career writing about simpler lifestyles, about the ways that the hyper-materialism of our culture leads not just to environmental trouble but also to a kind of spiritual emptiness, the substitution of accumulation for relationship, of shopping for experience. For years I've run a project through the Methodist Church that attempts to change the way people celebrate Christmas—$100 Holidays, it's called, and pastors urge their congregations to try to limit their spending on that level, one-tenth the American average, substituting homemade presents for store-bought, gifts of time and money for gifts of stuff. In fact, since it was November, I was spending many of the hours between ski runs on the phone, talking to reporters about Christmas, coordinating plans for alternative celebrations.

But much of the rest of the time, I was wandering the corridors of the Holiday Inn, drooling over gear, listening gravely as manufacturer's reps spun the wonder stories of their miracle garments. Here was the importer of Craft, an underwear with its own philosophy, its own Web site. "We are the Apple computers of underwear," he said, mysteriously. *An underwear worn by Björn Daehlie.* Here was the American head of the Rudy Project corporation, which makes the hottest new sunglasses, endlessly hotter than, say, old-fashioned Oakleys! Stefania Belmondo wore Rudy Project wraparounds! Here was a pallet full of tubes of Jogmate, a post-workout protein supplement that according to a Boston University study, "enhances muscle glycogen resynthesis," and in research at Vanderbilt was found to "enhance the recovery of leg protein stores." And to wash it down, rows of bottles of Pro Hydrator, a glycerol formulation that "pulls water deep into the cells and into the spaces between the cells," allowing you to "walk up to the starting line with several hundred more milliliters of fluid in your body than the person next to you."

I'd always loved cross-country skiing in part for its old-wool ethos—no need for the latest, sleekest, most neon. For a decade I'd skied in the same $35 L.L. Bean anorak, its front pouch encrusted with the ancient spume of a hundred tubes of wax. So why did I suddenly feel that I absolutely had to have—*had to have*—"a specialized weave of vaporizing polyester fibers that create a warm and constant microclimate next to the athlete's skin"? Why was I hanging around the Swix display, endlessly hefting their new carbon-fiber pole, so light you nearly couldn't feel it?

I rationalized thus: You have trained so hard and so long, why wouldn't you want the very best, the very fastest, the very lightest equipment on earth? If your new set of lungs lets you run half a mile an hour faster, maybe a new set of skis will do something similar. You whip that ski pole forward and back seventy times a minute—shaving an ounce off the end is like shaving four pounds a minute off your workload. In the course of a 50K race, that's almost half a ton. Whoa—think how tired you'd get trying to lift half a ton! What choice do you have?

More mystically, I couldn't help thinking of Björn Daehlie. Björn Daehlie wore this underwear. Doubtless he wore it because he was paid to—but he wore it and he won. I could share his microclimate, close to my skin! I didn't actually want his sweat; I wasn't that far gone. Brothers beneath the Lycra, though. I've always been baffled by the influence that celebrities wield over people's habits—why would anyone prefer a particular credit card or steak sauce because John Madden or Garth Brooks told them to? But now I had an idol too. Be like Björn!

Mostly, though, it was simply this: I finally understood something so well that I could appreciate what the finest gear was all about. I have a dear friend, a professional violinist, who is by no means rich, and yet will regularly and seriously contemplate spending fantastic sums—$20,000, say—for an instrument. In his case, the best technology is the oldest, but the principle is the same. He knows so well the subtle balances and tones and dynamics of a violin that he thirsts for the very best one. He doesn't need a great car because he's not a race car driver. A car is just his transportation. Even though I like to cook, I don't have any urge for the finest set of pots in the world. I wouldn't be able to really tell the difference between the taste of my dinner cooked in WonderPan and the taste of a dinner cooked in the stuff we got for our wedding.

The irony, of course, is that great skill can in fact overcome bad equipment. Mike sounds gorgeous on a mediocre violin; Björn Daehlie could take the first pair of wooden skis I owned as a kid, hitch the cable bindings to his hiking boots, and ski circles around almost anyone on earth. Still, it's sweet to dedicate yourself so completely to *anything* that you finally develop the sensitivity to really appreciate your gear. This is the exact opposite of the way advertisers would like you to approach the subject: Their unvarying refrain is that procuring the finest that your credit can command will let you more easily acquire the underlying skill. Buy a titanium bike and you will be able to climb any mountain! As a result, the garages of America bulge with gorgeous, unused gear. The skill comes only with the long hours; until you've built the calves and the reflexes, the titanium bike looks foolish on you. Till then you don't deserve the good stuff. And since any one of us is unlikely to get really good at more than a couple of things in the course of a lifetime, one can be anti-consumer and deeply materialist at the same time. In your small realms of real knowledge, materialism becomes an aesthetic. If we could confine it to those small realms, we'd be an elegant species.

That's what I told myself, anyhow. Man, those carbon-fiber poles were light!


By day three of my stay in West Yellowstone, the swiftest skis on earth couldn't have gotten me up the hills at the ski center. Suddenly I could barely climb the stairway to my hotel room. Luckily, it was right then that Ben Husaby appeared after driving all night from Oregon. He tossed his stuff on the next bed and took a worried look at my gray face. "Let me guess," he said. "You've been here three days." It turns out that the effects of altitude—West Yellowstone lies 6,666 feet above sea level—are purely predictable. For forty-eight hours, you feel fine, and then you don't. "Seasons can be broken here in Yellowstone," he said. "You can dig yourself so far under that you won't feel like getting out of bed for months." In fact, he continued, even at sea level training camp can be so exhausting that you've got to learn to take it easy. "One of the secrets to elite endurance athletics is the ability to stay in bed when you're not training," he said. "A prerequisite to a successful career is the ability to watch crappy TV for hours on end. I've known guys who could do it ten hours a day, just sit there and watch and rest."

Under his stern gaze, I spent the next two days skiing less and talking more—every meal offered whole-grain bagels, all-you-could-eat bananas, and endless talk about Nordic ski racing. But it was hard to pick out the elite racers—aside from the broad-shouldered Husaby, they looked utterly normal. Carl Swenson, for instance, is a Dartmouth philosophy grad who, at the age of twenty-eight, seemed to be reaching the top of his game. The previous winter he'd won the American Birkebeiner, the country's biggest race, something no Yank had managed for years. He also had become a dominant force in mountain bike racing, winning several stops on the NORBA circuit and helping pioneer the idea that someone could stay in top racing form nearly year-round. But he looked less like Superman than like—like a philosophy student at Dartmouth, small, slender, *normal*. I could usually find him at lunch next to Nathan Schultz, who also raced bikes all summer and skis all winter, and Erich Wilbrecht, a former biathlon champion making the slow transition into normal life at the age of thirty-eight. They could talk about anything—philosophy, say—but at my prodding they'd try to explain what racing felt like at the highest levels.

"The good days and the bad days seem to come out of thin air," Swenson said. "You can feel so damn good, and then everything can go wrong so damn quickly. When I'm going well, I've sort of had this confidence, but it's sort of like a superstition. You don't want to let yourself feel like that."

"When you warm up, if you feel terrible, that doesn't mean anything," added Schultz. "And if you feel great, that doesn't mean anything either."

"Hey—someone can be going great for forty kilometers," said Wilbrecht. "Then he starts to think about bacon cheeseburgers or something, and he just grinds to a halt."

"Here's what you've got to remember about skiing, and about mountain biking too," and Swenson. "It's not a long, steady effort like a running race. *It's a series of uphill sprints, and then recoveries on the downhills.* It's almost all-out to the top of each hill, regardless of the distance." That image stuck in my mind; it changed the way I understood what I was doing. I'd been thinking about racing as a faster version of the endless steady grind of training. But suddenly I understood the dynamic of a race differently, understood what I needed from my body, and understood exactly why it hurt the way it did. Precisely at the moment you would like to slow down, the moment you start to fight gravity as well as fatigue, you need to speed up. The hills are when the racing happens.

Unable to watch as much TV as Ben recommended, I'd been plowing through the adventures of one Gérard D'Abboville, "the man who braved the vast Pacific—and won!" His book describes rowing across the whole damn ocean, "a resistance fighter in a war I invented for myself, which I have to fight day after day, hour after hour, stroke after stroke, as each arc of the oars grows more difficult than the last." It was the thousand small temptations he had to fight: "to get out of bed five minutes later than usual, to pull a trifle less vigorously on the oar next time, the easings-off just a little here and there, which in and of themselves are insignificant, but when, taken together, ineluctably lead to the ultimate surrender." That was how I'd been thinking about racing—the one-foot-in-front-of-the-other waddle to the finish line. By now I knew I could handle that kind of hurt. But what about these uphill charges Swenson was describing? These racers seemed to be upping the stakes.

All year long, in the back of my mind, I'd known how far off Wednesday was, because Wednesday was interval day, the toughest hour of every week. In Rob's system, I did most of my intervals on hills—basically, I'd find the steepest pitch around and run or ski up as fast I could for four, six, eight, sometimes ten minutes. Then I'd jog back down and repeat, four or five or six times. The idea was to drive my heart right to its anaerobic threshold—about 165 beats per minute—and when I was doing intervals with real commitment that's what would happen. But it was easy, especially by the third or fourth interval, to begin backing off a bit. I'd need to pick a rock on a mountain trail and tell myself I had to touch it inside of six minutes; there was a particular birch on one of my wintertime ski hills that lay five hard minutes from the bottom of the hill. Intervals always seemed like mind games as much as anything else—could I force myself to push when I was really worn? But now I understood that the great racers saw their entire marathons as fifty kilometers' worth of intervals, except that in between hills they didn't jog, they galloped. Just thinking about it tired me out more than the Yellowstone altitude.

By day five, though, I was back out on the ski trails, slowly recovering my wind, working hard on my uphill technique. The coaches from the masters camps lined us wannabes up in long rows and watched our form as we slowly skied back and forth, diagnosing "late kick" and "bad weight transfer" and the other hitches that needed attention. The better skiers—the college hotshots, the national team members—weaved in and out of our groups, each pack in its color-coordinated Lycra. But the spirit on the trails were deeply democratic; it remained the most egalitarian of sports. I watched one day as a high school senior, a sectional champion on his first visit to West Yellowstone, lurched down the track, his wax grabbing snow and bringing him up short with every stride. Husaby, twice an Olympian, waved him over, took off the boy's skis, and proceeded to lick the wax with his tongue to warm it until it was soft enough to spread out in a thinner layer—he sent the kid away beaming.

And he was just as kind to me. On Thanksgiving morning, he woke up and announced that we were going to go for a ski into Yellowstone itself. Though the roads were officially closed, the rangers don't mind skiers using them as trails. So we ducked under the barriers, clipped in, and *went*. There was no need for wax at all; the road was icy, and the fastest way to ski was simply to double-pole—to hold your feet steady beneath you and do all the work with your arms and stomach, bending and pushing once a second or so. Ben was going slowly for him—he'd carry on conversations with other skiers as he passed them, point out elk lurking on the ridges—but I was right near the edge of my ability. I followed for twenty-five kilometers, to an intersection called Madison Junction, where we came across a friend of his and decided we'd take to the woods and meadows for a while.

As we skied more slowly, stopping to cross fallen logs and streamlets, we came upon a herd of perhaps three hundred bison. Their breath hung above the golden meadow; a coyote sat confidently on his haunches, surveying the scene; it was one of those rare moments when you wander into a calendar, when the sky is as blue and the snow as white and the air as clear and the animals as big and the mountains as high as you have always hoped. And it just got better. Ben had a particular hot pot he wanted to visit, but it lay on the other side of the Gibbon River, about a mile above its confluence with the Firehole River. So we stripped down to skivvies, took the insoles out of our ski boots and put them inside our socks, and waded the thigh-deep snowmelt. It was 15 degrees out, but the sun was still just high enough to warm us as we dressed on the far side. We climbed out to the steaming pool, and then finally back to the road, back into the skis, for twenty-four more kilometers of double-poling back to town. Except for a couple of buffalo who chased us a few hundred yards, there wasn't much drama, just the endless pumping to keep up with Ben. But it was sublime nonetheless. The sun dropped over the ridges, the tall grass casting shadows on the thin snow. And I kept going, kept going, kept going. Small hills would loom before me, and I'd top them with relative ease; Ben's back stayed in sight; if my arms ached it made no difference.

I knew that a year before I couldn't have done this, or anything like it—that I wouldn't have had the confidence to even give it a try. Fifty kilometers is a long way to travel on the strength of your triceps and your stomach and your will. We finally made it back under the park barrier as dusk began to gather, and Ben said, "You did all right. You showed me some mettle." Which was sweet of him to say, but for once in my life I hardly needed it. I knew I'd done okay.

# 14

I was home the next day, for our slightly rescheduled Thanksgiving, with Dad presiding silently but cheerfully at the head of the table. We convinced ourselves we had much to be thankful for, and all was joy.

After the turkey settled, I went for a run, and instantly understood why athletes are so eager to train at altitude. My body had compensated for the thinner air by adding extra red blood cells so that it could carry a normal volume of oxygen to my muscles. Those extra cells were still in my system, but now the air was oxygen-rich once more, so I had an extra dose of energy circulating with every breath. I ran through the streets of suburban Boston on a high—no matter how hard I pushed, I couldn't make myself hurt. So *this* is why endurance athletes had tried blood-doping over the years, why the Tour de France ran on the synthetic blood thickener EPO, why the great cross-country skiers now lived in special pressurized houses that made them feel as if they inhabited the Himalayas. My heart rate monitor showed I was working reasonably hard, my heart beating more than 150 times a minute, but I could have been out for the lightest of jogs. I felt out ahead of my body, filled with so much energy I was nearly outrunning my feet.

Sadly, the corpuscles quickly disappeared, and with them the sense that I had become a minor deity. Worse than that, the East was still warm and bare as December began. The snow in the Rockies had spoiled me; the last thing I wanted now was to be running on pavement. The temperature hit the 70s on the first of the month; the pond by our house, normally full of skaters by Thanksgiving, was full of summery ripples. No need for the woodstove; we slept with the windows open.

It bothered me on many levels. For ten years I'd been a nearly full-time student of global warming, writing one of the first books on the subject and following it up with hundreds of speeches and articles; 1998 was supposed to be a vacation from all that. But in early December, NASA published figures predicting that 1998 would enter the record books by far the warmest year in human history. All that warm air, which holds more water vapor than cold, had brought devastation around the globe: Wild floods had turned 300 million people into refugees for a week, for a month, forever, as the Yangtze had surged across China, the Brahmaputra across Bangladesh. In other places, the hot air had increased evaporation and hence brought drought—whole counties in Florida were evacuated in the face of forest fires. Insurers later calculated that 1998 cost them $96 billion in claims, more than half again as much as any year on record. Scientists published papers showing that birds and butterflies were changing their migration patterns and their ranges. It was the year it finally became apparent just how much damage human beings had done to the world's climate, and hence to everything that happens on the surface of the planet.

I spent years worrying about such things, tracking the rising sea temperatures that were bleaching coral reefs, writing about the increase in the strength and frequency of hurricanes. But I felt it most personally come winter. Always my favorite of seasons, it had become deeply unreliable in the past ten years. As the man from Fischer Skis had said, global warming had already damaged their business, interrupting every winter with long stretches of mud and thaw. Business would doubtless carry on; in fact, I'd just come across a series of economic forecasts proving, in the smug fashion of economists, that increases in the greens fees from golfers would outweigh the loss from declining ski sales. But I didn't want to play golf—I wanted to speed sublimely through the woods, riding on an outstretched ski, pushing with every muscle in my body. I wanted the annual remission from friction.

I wanted it badly enough that on the 8th of December, my thirty-eighth birthday, I came back from a long, hot run and jumped into the pond. Not for a swim—it *was* too cold to stay more than a few seconds—but just to thumb my nose at the weather gods and make them send winter. And the next day, by God, it actually snowed. Of course, it snowed only an inch, exquisite tiny flakes feathering like dust on the cruciform branches of the hemlocks. But it was just enough to lure me out on my new refinished skis, which I immediately scraped on some gravel, damaging the bases.

At least the damage gave me something to work on. Every night after dinner, as soon as Sophie went to bed, I'd repair to the bench in my workshop, fire up my special waxing iron, and get to work. Prepping skis for racing requires more than picking the right kick wax the day of the race. You also need to endlessly polish the tips and tails to create maximum glide. You brush them with a brass brush, slowly melt a layer of wax into the base, wait half an hour for it to cool, scrape it all off, and begin again. Each time, your ski gets infinitesimally faster. "What it takes to prepare a pair of skis is just absurd," John Broadhead, the masters champion, said one day. "But you have to do it—it's so frustrating to stick with some guy right up a hill, then tuck in behind him on the downhill and watch him sail away because his skis are slicker." After a while he added, "It acquires a religious ritual aspect— applying mysterious ointments in semi-mystical sequences, then scraping them all away leaving . . . nothing. Nothing visible any- way. It's a kind of prayer."

Once I'd run the beads on this peculiar rosary, I'd head upstairs to my office and do what any self-respecting modern would do in such a situation—search the Web for hours, tracking down miscel- laneous information from snowier corners of the far-flung Nordic world. If you don't read Norwegian, there aren't that many Web sites to choose from, and by far the best is fasterskier.com, serving American aficionados for a full five years with training tips, a workout of the week, and news updates. This just in: The Norwe- gian wax technician has defected to the Swedish team, and dark rumors abound that he has taken secret potions with him—ninety kilos of something or another, no one's sure what. And maybe some test skis. Uproar and unhappiness! On the one hand, the Norwegians are loath to admit that any of their dominance comes from chemicals, even chemicals applied to the bottoms of their skis. On the other hand, the Swedes are their great rivals, the Red

Sox to their Yankees. Not only that, but one of Norway's top women was disqualified from a race because her blood had too much hemoglobin—apparently she'd spent too much time in Daehlie's special "altitude house," his Himalayas-in-a-Winnebago. But then Björn himself calmed the waters by winning the first World Cup race of the year, and the fortieth of his career. According to the translated version of the Oslo sports section, he remarked that "after 3.5 kilometers I fell in the downhill slope very unnecessary and I became irritated. After that I had to struggle like an animal all the way." Meanwhile, closer to home, it appeared that Oregon star Justin Wadsworth has, yes, switched to Atomic skis from Rossignols. "I felt the time was right for a change," explained Wadsworth patiently. What did we do before the Internet?

Still, if you hunted hard enough, there was some real writing. I'd become addicted to a Web site updated each day by up-and-coming racer Cory Smith. He calls it "Somewhere Between Obscurity and Oblivion," an apt description of the existence of an American Nordic contender, and offers accounts of each of his training sessions and races, not to mention top ten lists of his best injuries, biggest meals, and so on. Forget Showercam—this is voyeurism on a high plane. One day will see a breakthrough: Videotape analysis has demonstrated that he is planting his poles a few inches too far back, "next to my boot rather than in front of it." The next day something will go wrong: With the temperature dropping and the wrong wax on his skis, he fights up the first hill of a race only to watch as six skiers with faster boards glide right by on the downhill: "I felt like a child who had worked so hard to build a beautiful sandcastle, only to watch helplessly as the tide washed it away before it was finished."

Another young racer, Kurt Wulff, was sending back Web reports from Norway, where he'd gone to ski full-time for a couple of years. "All my life I have wanted to be the best," he writes. Having finished college, and without a slot on the national team to give him a structure for training, he decided his best hope was a move to Scandinavia. "It would be irresponsible to say the only way to become a fast ski racer is to come to Norway; however, I firmly believe that it is the only way for me." He's living in a Trondheim apartment next to Frode Estil, sometimes touted as the next you-know-who, studying Norwegian, and skiing, skiing, skiing, his results improving by the week. By midwinter he was "blending my spirituality, nature, my school, my training, my racing, composing a lifestyle in which all of my important aspects can thrive. I live in Norway. I am an American. I love it!"

Inspired by all that enthusiasm, I clicked a button I'd been avoiding for months. Rob had been pushing me to pick a final race to aim for, something grand enough to be worthy of this whole experiment—he'd been urging me to think about the Norwegian Birkebeiner, held each March on a course that runs over the mountains from Rena to Lillehammer. The mother of all cross-country races, it commemorates the pivotal event in a thirteen-century civil war. The Birkebeiners—Birchleggers—were the underdogs, "often in such dire need that they had nothing but the bark of birch trees as footwear." But they were determined that the rival faction, the Baglers, not capture Haakon Haakonsson, the toddler son of their dying king. So on Christmas day 1205, two of the best Birkebeiner skiers spirited him away in an epic journey across the mountains, "suffering much from the cold, snow, and wind" in the process. The boy grew up to be King Haakon, and to finally rout the Baglers, raising Norway to its medieval glory. And hence, each year, Norwegian skiers retrace the route across the mountains. Fifty-eight kilometers across the mountains, which is about forty miles, which is a long ways, especially since it's mostly uphill, and especially since all entrants need to carry an eight pound pack on their backs the entire way, to match the weight of the young kind.

I doubted I'd be able to go. With Dad dying, the prospect of a transatlantic trip seemed unlikely. And I wondered if I could even finish the race—back at trusty fasterskier.com I found a firsthand account of last year's race from an American masters skier, and it sounded truly nasty. "The first 15 kilometers are nothing but climbing," he reported. "Breaking rocks on a chain gang would probably have been easier. UP-UP-UP-UP!!" By the time he'd skied forty-five minutes, he'd already climbed 1,850 feet, and he had thirty-eight kilometers left to go. "When I was coherent, the views from the top of the mountains were spectacular; however, that wasn't too often. I would have grabbed some energy bars out of my pack, but I didn't have the energy to do it! Basically, it was the hardest race I had ever participated in."

The computer even offered me a profile of the course, showing every climb along the way. I stared at the image long enough to engrave it on my cortex, and I clicked the button for an application. Maybe Dad would get better for a while—maybe the "good time" would arrive—and I'd be able to go. I knew I *wanted* to; it sounded crazy, hard enough to justify this crazy year.

This crazy year in which winter seemed never to come. By mid-December we'd set up the Christmas tree at church and gone caroling in shirtsleeves. I kept running, long treks across the unfrozen mountain trails. Every few days some rumor of a cold front would come across the radio—"chance of snow on Thursday"—

but Thursday would bring, at best, a cold drizzle. I could feel my body champing at the bit. As the workouts on my schedule began to shorten a little, my body didn't drain itself of energy every day. I sensed my readiness to race, which only drove me nuttier with each clear, warm day.

Finally, December 17 brought a little snow to the Adirondacks. Not quite enough to ski on in the backyard, but a few phone calls established that the Olympic trails at Lake Placid were partially open. They were barely covered—"fast grass," one of the locals called it—but it was skiing. I had it to myself for a couple of hours, around and around the same short loops, and then kids starting arriving. The local biathletes, guns strapped to their backs; the masters skiers; everyone who was desperate for snow. The next day it was gone—warm, foggy air melted big tawny patches in the snow, and it was back to the damn Nordic-Track. And then it rained all night, the steady drum of water against the tin roof. I stayed awake half the night calculating just how much snow would be piling up if the temperature were ten degrees colder.

For a year I'd been readying myself for a sixteen-week window of snow: December, January, February, March. Now December was pretty well shot; the Northeast was still brown.

Except for the gerbil wheel.

The winter before I'd met some Boston skiers at one of the races, and they'd told me how they stayed in form through the city's on-and-off winters. Just outside of town, at the confluence of the Mass Pike and Route 128, on a public golf course in the town of Weston, the local authorities maintained a few snow guns. When the temperature dropped below freezing, they coated the area around the eighteenth hole, groomed it out nice and flat, and then charged $10 a head. Mostly they attracted local families looking for something new to do on the weekend—small children tottered back and forth in the granular snow. But the racers were there too—college kids on holiday break, the masters skiers tuning up for the races in northern New England later in the winter. And since I was spending much of the month in Boston at my parents' house, I found my way to the gerbil wheel too.

The loop covered about a half kilometer; at a nice easy pace you could ski it in two minutes. On every side lay sodden brown golf course. The loop climbed one "hill," perhaps twelve feet high, and fell back down the other side. No flickering shadows through the pine needles as you flew by, no owls high in the branches watching, no squeak of powder, no tracks disappearing into the distance. It was to cross-country skiing as your kitchen tap is to Niagara Falls, as Central Park is to Central America. I didn't even *believe* in man-made snow, any more than I believed in chairlifts—that's one of the reasons I loved cross-country skiing. It was supposed to be *organic*.

But as Christmas neared, the gerbil wheel was where you could find me. Pinned to the bulletin board in the clubhouse, right underneath the notices about greens fees and tee times, I found a few faxes from other ski areas around the Northeast, all of them offering special holiday packages, but admitting they still had no snow. Groups of skiers, sweaty in their Lycra after workouts in the humid air, stood around discussing rumors of snow like high school kids speculating where they might buy pot. Short of air travel, they were out of luck. You could drive straight to the Canadian border and not find conditions to match this half-kilometer track.

It became my refuge from a house grown increasingly tense. We got through Christmas Day just fine—a lot of the ornaments hung at wheelchair height, testament to Dad's pleasure in the work—but then things began to fall apart a little. Tired from the strain of this last big celebration, Dad was all but comatose for a couple of days. We had to take him to the hospital for another MRI, this one to see what the radiation had accomplished, but he was listing so badly to the left we barely got him inside the chair car for the ride. After the usual long delays, the doctors appeared to meet with us all. The tests, they said, showed his tumor had responded to the radiation and shrunk a little. This should be the "good time"; they weren't sure why he was so groggy, unless maybe all the radiation had taken its own toll. They doubted he'd get any better; eventually the tumor would regrow. "Were it my dad," said the surgeon, "I wouldn't do much more."

At which point Dad emerged from his fog for the first time all day to ask yet again that he be treated "aggressively." Which annoyed the hell out of me—some part of me wanted him to go away and stop bothering us. Stop making me feel guilty for not being more help to my mother; stop pulling me away from my family; stop stop stop being so damn needy, so unlike my father. Which, of course, left me feeling twice as guilty as before. We'd all been pointing toward Christmas, to having one last real celebration. But now what did we point toward?

A snowstorm might have righted me; it usually does. A couple of hours alone in the deep woods gliding along, pushing up hills and carving down them, breaking out into the open on Adirondack lakes, tucking back into the hemlock woods, reminding me of the proper order and scale of things. But now even the instasnow at the gerbil track was melting as the temperature climbed.

Back on the Internet, the only consolation I could find was an article by Bill Koch, the Nordic legend, about his experiments with beach-skiing. The best place to beach-ski is right at the froth line, where the sand stays slightly wet, he reported; there it's possible to reach speeds equal to most snow conditions. And you don't even need to wax. Though mid-western beaches can wear through a ski base in a season, the fine sands of Hawaii don't wear out your skis any more than snow. "And best of all you can take off your skis and go swimming when you're done." Another week like this, and I'd be headed to Cape Cod.

## 15

Be careful what you wish for. When winter came, it came whistling.

On the first night of the new year, exactly a year after my training had begun, I was driving west from the Adirondacks toward the Tug Hill Plateau for the first race of the season. According to the thermometer on the dashboard, the temperature was dropping steadily: five below, eight below, eleven below, sixteen below, the kind of dry cold that insinuates itself through the closed windows of the car, the kind that sticks your nostrils together when you stand outside and take a breath. I checked into a motel, drank gallons of water, and tried to sleep.

It was bitter and clear when the sun came up, and the farther I drove into the plateau the higher the snowbanks got. Virtually every vehicle that passed me pulled a trailer with a Ski-Doo or two on the back—the snowmobilers were obviously as snow-starved as the skiers, and far more numerous. Today's race was a small contest on a distant course; it drew perhaps seventy-five skiers ready to go ten kilometers, and nearly all of them were young guys, college racers at the end of their holiday break or kids a couple of years out of school and still in race shape. Their nonchalant speed intimidated me, and so did the cold: I tried "warming up," but only got colder, so I retreated inside the one small shack and waited for my start time. I tried to "visualize" and foresaw humiliation.

Instead of the mass starts I was used to, the organizers sent racers out of the chute one by one, every thirty seconds. Which meant that half a minute after you'd begun, someone was on your tail, hunting you down. Before I was halfway done with the first five-kilometer loop, they'd begun to pass me, quickly and efficiently. I'd never skied a race this short—I had no idea how to pace myself, and with my discombobulation any sense of rhythm disappeared. Instead of focusing on technique, I could hear my mind singing me the same old song about how awkward I was. I flailed, windmilling my way up the hills, gasping. It's hard to imagine that you can feel so different, one day to the next, when your body is doing basically the same thing. I'm sure that from the outside I looked no clumsier than usual. But I spent the whole half hour of the race feeling as if I was behind my skis, trying to catch up with them. None of that centered, up-on-top powerful feeling. It had all come too fast; 1999, winter; the end of the race. As if I hadn't had time to get in gear.

The next day, training at our local ski area, Garnet Hill, I came around a corner and saw a flash of blond hair that I knew belonged to Doug Diehl, one of the top finishers from the day before. He'd blown by me two kilometers from the finish. Probably the best skier on the local tracks, he never missed a workout—in December, he'd been chased off one of the local golf courses where he was trying to ski the frozen grass, so he'd headed for the base area of the nearest downhill area and skied loops around the bottom of the lift lines on the man-made powder. He let me slip in behind him to copy his graceful technique, and he started talking about how he'd been doing basically this for fifteen years, day in and day out. For the first four, he'd been a straggler, running in the middle of the pack. "It takes a long while to build the base, and for the muscles to learn how to fire." But he trained patiently—he, too, walked up the hills to keep his heart rate low—and now he had the times to show for it: He'd finished yesterday's 10K in 31:45, three or four minutes faster than I. That the best World Cup skiers could cover the same ground in twenty-six minutes seemed almost inconceivable—they hadn't been training much longer or harder. "They're anaerobic mutants," he muttered. It reminded me I was somewhere along a continuum, with the happy-just-to-finish at one end, Doug and I strung out somewhere in the middle, and Björn at the top. It reminded me I wasn't trying to win, that I couldn't be embarrassed by slow times.

It also reminded me that I had set one goal for myself, and that was to give a supreme effort sometime this winter. That at least was still in reach.


I was yo-yoing back and forth between the Adirondacks and Boston, five hours' drive on the Adirondack Northway and the relentlessly straight Mass Pike, too much time to think. Dad was weakening, what little coordination he still possessed failing him. He could no longer scoot himself to the edge of the bed to be slid into his wheelchair, so the Hoyer lift trundled into our lives. A Hoyer lift is a kind of derrick. Dad now lay on a grommeted blanket, and when the time came to leave the bed we would attach chains to the grommets and winch him up, swing him through the air, and settle him into the wheelchair. He was still gaining weight—the steroids that kept the swelling down in his brain also added bulk to his body—and Mom looked like a longshoreman as she maneuvered this six-foot-three cargo through the air twice a day. Somehow she'd kept body and soul together, though she'd rarely left the house since he came home from the hospital; even when aids arrived to help change him, she stayed by his side, making sure they were gentle enough.

One day, though, I convinced her to go out shopping, and Dad and I just sat in his room and talked. I asked him if he knew what was wrong with him, and he confessed that he couldn't remember where the tumor was. "Your brain," I said, trying to sound calm and controlled. It's in both halves, I added.

"That doesn't sound too hopeful," he said, and I realized he was fishing for clues about his situation.

And so I told him again, slowly and without sugar, what the doctors had told him a few weeks before after his MRI. He had perhaps four months and then the tumor would regrow "and that would be near the end."

He looked somber, paused for a moment as if taking it in, and then thanked me for telling him "more directly than I've heard it in the past."

I had no idea if I wanted him to remember or not. How cruel to relive the moment of your death sentence every few days, each time afresh; how sweet not to marinate in your own finality each moment of your last few months. I told him because I was his elder son and owed him respect, not protection. And because I knew he could handle it. His dignity somehow grew with each day that passed—not pride, but its opposite, the dignity of someone untroubled by pride. His days consisted mostly of inputs and outputs, fistfuls of pills and carefully measured urine spilling into his catheter bag, morning enemas and evening cleanings. It could have been horrible, but he did not complain, he was not long-suffering, he just got through it, and thanked everyone for their help. He was gracious, easy to be with, even though he rarely talked much. His dignity did not reside in his body—that was a clue for me as I thought about the meaning of my endless exercise. His strength came from somewhere else, and I did not know quite where. Not the easy assurances of religion; he enjoyed the visits of the young preacher who had taken on his case, but he wanted him to talk about sports or the newspaper, not heaven. Not a desire for death; he never once betrayed an impatience with his condition. The closest he got to philosophy was another day when Mom had left the house. "I guess I'm the kind of person who, if I've given it a good shot, can deal with what comes," he said, without a trace of bravado. I still didn't know what kind of person that was, but I knew he spoke the truth about himself.

As for me, I seemed to be going in a new direction every day. I'd wake up feeling strong and go out and ski a series of hard uphill intervals with relaxed intensity; on the last of six eight-minute uphill climbs, just as I was getting bone-tired, the grooming machine suddenly appeared on the trail behind me, horn honking. Rather than pull over and let it pass, I decided to race it up the hill, never looking back—my heart shot through the roof, but I was laughing as hard as the guys in the groomer. A few days later, though, I'd pull on my tights for the same workout and have to grit my teeth through each repeat, looking for any excuse to drop the pace, finish early. The weather stayed terrible across the country, as one race after another was canceled for lack of snow; in our mountainous pocket we had just enough to ski on, but the race we'd all been pointing toward, the Lake Placid Loppet, was called off not once but twice due to the snow drought.

I decided to head back to Craftsbury, a year to the week after the first race of my life, for the annual marathon. I'd go 25K, twice around the course that most of the field would circle four times. A friend lent me his cabin in the woods, and after a wrenching day in Boston I headed up alone, falling asleep in a gorgeous whirling snowstorm. When I crawled out from under the quilts the next morning and set about stoking the stove and cooking my oatmeal, I felt ready, strong. By the time I reached the racecourse, I knew my wax wasn't working perfectly, but I didn't care; the Factory Team guys were on hand for the race and full of cheerful chat. They leapt off the line when the cowbell rang, skating hard for the lead against a team from Rossignol; I stayed at the back of the pack, per my plan, trying to start slowly and not repeat the overeager launch that sabotaged my Australian race.

But a funny thing happened—I never speeded up. It was as if I'd forgotten the point of racing. I'd pass some people, mostly the much-older masters skiers, but I could have been out for a leisurely ski. I knew it was happening, and I'd tell myself to pick it up, to Go Go Go. For a hundred yards my tempo would build, and then I'd relax again, lose my focus, settle back into the skiing equivalent of a fast trot. I felt abstracted from the whole business, as if I were watching myself ski. The world seemed muffled, foggy, with none of the heightened perception I'd noticed in other races. At the very end, on a grueling three-kilometer uphill, I finally managed to make myself work, mostly because I feared that the fast skiers were about to lap me, which would have been truly humiliating. I finished my second and final lap in 1:56, thirty seconds ahead of Carl Swenson as he came around for the *third* time on his way to the full 50K distance. I offered a feeble cheer, peeled off my barely sweaty Lycra suit, and wandered off to help Andrew Gerlach, the Factory Team manager, who was handing water bottles to his athletes as they came by on their final lap.

Away from my dreamy saunter, he reported, it had been a wild race. Most of the Rossignol skiers had gone out very fast, forcing Swenson to hold their pace. Then, unexpectedly, they'd dropped out after twenty-five kilometers, apparently hoping they'd set him up to be taken by Chris Blanchard, their Canadian star. The two of them were far in front of the field, according to the reports coming in by radio from around the field; they were clearly saving themselves for a sprint to the finish. When it came, it was almost anticlimactic. They broke into sight a quarter mile from the tape, side by side, but then Swenson pulled easily away, hardly a trace of effort on his face. When he crossed the line, he took a few deep breaths, and then turned to me and said, "Hey, how was your race?"

A good question. What on earth was wrong? It marked the low point of the whole experiment—I'd gone faster twelve months earlier on two weeks of training. When I e-mailed Rob with news of my lackadaisical showing, he said, as usual, not to worry—my program was pitched to make me peak a month later, as February turned into March. But, again, as after Australia, I doubted my legs were the problem. A few days later I happened to be working out in a gym when ESPN interrupted its regular programming to offer live coverage of Michael Jordan's retirement announcement. It wasn't the physical demands that were driving him out of the sport, he said, but the sense that he "couldn't count on [himself] to get excited for every game any more." I'd never paid much attention to the banalities athletes serve up once they've been asked the same questions a thousand times, but what he said hit home. Think how hard it would be to really get up for a game, night after night, year after year. At some point it would stop seeming important; ego or professionalism or a love for the sheer aesthetic beauty of the game might keep you going quite awhile, but how much more work it would be once the excitement faded away.

An overlong career clearly didn't account for my apathy, of course—the Craftsbury debacle had been my sixth, count 'em, race. My mind was just elsewhere, on a struggle far more absorbing and demanding. It occurred to me again that I should just drop this whole experiment and forget about skiing for a while. One day, in fact, I blew off the intervals that Rob had scheduled, only the second time in a year I'd missed my workout. But the thought of stopping panicked me; what structure my life retained came from the computer printout sitting on my desk with the daily demand for exercise. And some days it still worked—I'd find myself bulling along, snorting frosty steam, and realize I'd been skiing for two hours, deep in some world inside me, relaxed and calm.

Sometimes it even seemed as if Rob was right, as if my body was rounding into shape right on schedule, as if all the cycles he'd so meticulously programmed thirteen months before had done their job. I skied a time trial late in the month, pushing myself hard through a fifteen-kilometer course. By any measure I was still slow—barely under four minutes a kilometer—but I'd felt free and easy; I wasn't spent at the end.

A couple of days later, whipping around the same trails, I crossed a pole in front of a ski on a tight corner and fell with all my weight on my right thumb, bending it back against my wrist. Hurt like hell, and I was too stupid to stop; by the time I came in from a series of speed drills the thumb was so swollen I could barely take my glove off, and when I did it was a cartoon shade of purple. I flashed back to Michael Jordan's press conference. Just as I'd never completely understood about being up for a game, I'd also never quite gotten it when athletes worried about nagging injuries. Now I knew—I alternated between wanting to let my thumb rest completely so that it would heal and wanting constantly to test it, to see how it was doing.

The bad news was that all my skiing pals said they'd seen the same kind of injury dozens of times—skiers' thumb, it's sometimes called, because the way a skier grips a pole leaves him vulnerable. It takes months to heal, they assured me. The good news was, once I painfully maneuvered it inside my mitten, it didn't hurt much when I skied. And the *really* good news, which almost made it all worthwhile, came when I visited the doctor for an x-ray. She started by checking my pulse and my blood pressure; having taken them once, she took them again, and then she asked me, "Are you an athlete?" Oh well, I said, I guess. Sort of. Yeah.

# 16

We celebrated Dad's birthday late in January, and he maintained enough coordination to take a whack at the piñata from his wheelchair, and enough good humor to laugh when he missed. That night I had a long, involved dream, and when I woke I could remember a single scene. Dad was up and walking around—in fact he was backpedaling to take a photo of the family. There was a suitcase on the ground behind him, and we were all terrified he was about to trip over it, when, without a glance, he skipped around it à la Fred Astaire. I was grinning when I woke up, and the grin didn't fade. It's not that I thought it an omen of some miraculous recovery. It just proved to me that when he was gone I'd be able to remember him as he'd been, not just as he was now.

In real life, Dad was setting off on some major journey. With each day that passed, he seemed to grow a bit more abstracted from the world around him—a world that had now evaporated down to his family and the aides who came to help turn him, clean him, and on good days hoist him into his wheelchair for an hour or two. He was never short with any of us, never waved off his meals or his cleanings, though they were often painful and tiring. If his grand-children were on hand, he would watch them playing around his bed with deep delight, and he never ceased following Mom with his eyes. But he was spending more and more of each day in some different world, and sometimes I felt almost guilty when we had to summon him back to the here-and-now for pills and enemas or whatever the daily round demanded.

He talked less and less, usually only in response to questions. Sometimes the world he was visiting seemed inscrutable. Once I asked him what he was thinking so deeply about, and he replied, in a loud voice, "Insects!" But he did tell Mom several times that he constantly saw a white line in front of his eyes. One morning, when he was more alert than usual and when we had the house to ourselves, I asked him if he could describe the line to me. He asked for a pencil and, gripping it tightly in his shaking hand, drew a wavering line about two-thirds of the way across the page and labeled it R. On the edge of the paper, he drew a wavering circle and with great effort wrote "W. Ocean" across it. (In a lifetime of writing, they were the last words he ever wrote.) The picture represented, he said, a "typical western river" leading to a "western ocean."

"And what does that ocean mean?" I asked.

"Infinity," he said. "Completeness."

He nodded off for a few moments and then woke back up. Why didn't the river connect to the ocean? I asked.

There were, he said, necessary tasks still to be done, but he couldn't find the words to say what they were.

"Is death more scary to think about or more peaceful?" I asked.

"More peaceful," he said emphatically, and then drifted back to sleep.

This time, when he woke up, I'd fetched a copy of *The Voyage of the Dawn Treader*; one of the C. S. Lewis Chronicles of Narnia, which is my boyhood he had read aloud every night after dinner till we'd gone through the series twice. This time I read to him, from the very end of the book, where the children, and Reepicheep the mouse, have sailed off toward the edge of the world: "There was no need to row, for the current drifted them steadily to the east. None of them slept or ate. All that night and all next day they glided eastward, and when the third day dawned they saw a wonder ahead. It was as if a wall stood up between them and the sky, a greenish-gray, trembling, shimmering wall. Then up came the sun, and at its first rising they saw it through the wall and it turned into wonderful rainbow colors . . .. What they saw beyond the sun was a range of montains. It was so high that either they never saw the top of it, or they forgot it."

He nodded sagely, as if the words were as clear and obvious as a newspaper story, and then he went off to sleep again. That night at dinner he seemed happy—we'd been discussing "ultimate truths," he told Mom, with just a little smile to let us know he knew how unlike him it was to discuss ultimate truths. But a new he was clearly taking shape before our eyes.


My own journey seemed all but irrelevant, dull even to me compared with the drama now playing in the house where I'd grown up, but by now the training was so ingrained that I kept with it almost automatically. And Rob, the one person besides my wife whom I'd trusted with my resolve to mount a supreme effort in some race, kept trying to help me find the right venue.

The trip of Lillehammer seemed less likely than ever, but I came across a brochure for this year's Keskinada races in Ottawa. The theme for 1999 was "Norway"; they were trying to duplicate parts of the Birkebeiner in Canada, including sending off one wave of racers carrying eight-pound backpacks, just as in the Norwegian race. I figured I could manage a weekend in Ottawa, a quick plane flight from Boston if need be, and so the images that started to fill my mind while I trained were suddenly Canadian: the pine forests of the Gatineau Park, the fifty-kilometer trail.

Rob told me to prepare with a four-hour time trial two weeks before the race, just to get my body used to staying out there that long, and so I set aside a Saturday, laid out my ski clothes, went to bed early. But as I was climbing out of bed in the early-morning darkness, the phone rang: Mom calling to say that she hadn't been able to rouse Dad that morning, that they were taking him to the hospital. I spent the morning by the phone, rattled. A few hours later she called to say that they'd increased his dose of steroids, apparently reducing the swelling in his brain a bit, and he had rallied. They were now giving him as many steroids as his body could tolerate, so there was no fallback for the next time it happened, but for the moment he was stabilized.

I headed out for my ski, and on the way over turned on the car radio, which was broadcasting the endless and useless impeachment debate in the Senate, a subject I had long since ceased to care even slightly about. But that day the start of the proceedings were delayed; it seemed that the clerk of the Senate, who had been reading the charges in his booming voice only the day before, had been killed by a car that night while walking with his wife to dinner. For whatever reason—the sheer goddamn vulnerability of humans, thinking of dinner one minute and dead the next—it made me unbearably sad. Tears were rolling down my cheek, and I just turned around and headed for home.

I got up the next day, though, checked in with home to make sure Dad was still breathing, and then headed off to the ski tracks for my four-hour test. Four hours is a long time, especially with none of the adrenaline of a race to distract you; I did the same five-kilometer loop eleven times, till I knew every soft spot in the snow. Every lap brought me by a pigpen filled with noisy hogs; I'd stop there and down some water and a Clif Shot, an "energy gel" that you squeeze like toothpaste into your mouth and try to swallow. It kept me going, not especially fast but perfectly reliably. When the clock finally stopped, I'd gone fifty-five kilometers, and proved to myself that at the very least I could manage the distances in the races ahead. And I'd done it with my pack on my back, like a true Birchlegger.

Almost in spite of myself, in fact, I could feel my body starting to peak. As the really long workouts of the fall dwindled in number and distance, and the brutal intervals built up my speed, power began to accumulate. I imagined that I knew what a racehorse felt like in the gate, pent-up energy ready to express itself. Long, hard uphill skiing left me feeling spent but not wasted; my body craved fuel and burned it evenly; I was eager for a test, impatient for the Ottawa race to arrive. I was, in fact, in the best physical shape of my life.

In the middle of all this, my friend John Race arrived for a visit. We'd met when he guided me up Mount Rainier five years before. He'd taken me back to the top a couple of summers later by a different route; we'd traded visits, become friends. I was always happy to see him because he'd come at the world through such a different path. Intellectually curious the way I was physically curious, he'd nonetheless spent almost all his energy on things of the body and the spirit. A rock and ice climber from adolescence, he'd graduated to big mountain expedition climbing before he was even out of college—he'd spent months on Denali, gotten within five hundred feet of the top of Everest, climbed 26,000-foot peaks like Cho Oyu. And he'd had to watch as friends died. He'd had to come to terms with the possibility he'd die himself up in those extreme lands. Now he was hungry for intellectual growth—he'd taught himself to run a guiding business and a summer backpacking program for high school kids, and he wanted to write about his experiences. He was busy playing on the path I'd been following since I could first remember, and I was busy playing on his. It made me think once more of Rob's first notion—each of us born to be balanced physically, intellectually, and spiritually. "It can happen simultaneously, but you also have a whole lifetime," Rob had said.

It hadn't taken me long to figure out how linked all three could be. If exercise was about being physical, then racing—being willing to hurt, to go harder than you wanted too—had an obvious spiritual quality. But the neat progression of my idea ran into trouble when Dad got sick. He was clearly now operating at some higher level, but it *wasn't* because he was trying. Instead, it seemed to be because he was letting go. Not giving up, not dropping out, but slowly, methodically, patiently letting go of his life. Talking got harder and harder for him, and often I would just sit and read him the newspaper, or chatter about my life. Every so often, though, I kept trying to ask serious questions, to find out what was going on inside. Partly it was just my curiosity—I'd never been so close before to someone who was very nearly dead. But I sensed, too, that he enjoyed talking about it, liked the fact that someone acknowledged he was dying and that it was an interesting process. One day he muttered that he was trying to figure out if there was something beyond this "make-believe" world, if there was something beyond "next week." When we watched TV he would try to explain to me that there was something odd about it. The tumor had robbed him of too much of his vocabulary to let him make his objection clear, but I knew that he was sensing its unreal absurdity on a new level. His metaphors, like the drawing of the river, tended always toward the outdoor, the concrete, toward the joys of the western boyhood that had filled his imagination ever since. "I feel like I'm climbing," he told me slowly one day. "Like I'm climbing up a cliff."

"Are you near the top?" I asked.

"Getting there," he said, with a grin.

It made me very glad we'd shared a life of climbing mountains, because I knew not to misinterpret his words. Climbing wasn't a struggle for him, didn't represent a battle or even a test. Climbing was a great joy, because it carried you higher, to where the view was clearer. I thought of all the climbs we'd taken when I was young, in the mountains of Maine and New Hampshire; I thought of the pleasure he'd taken in the Adirondacks when I moved there; I thought most of all of the long trip we'd taken with his brother and my brother around the Wonderland Trail that circles Mount Rainier. Some days had been tough. One morning we'd woken up, in mid-July, in a raging snowstorm, and hiked out seventeen tough miles to reach the road. But every time I'd looked at him in that couple of weeks, he'd been grinning. And nowhere more than on the long climbs after crossing one of the glacial valleys. Though the grand views may have started you slogging in the first place, no one kept hiking for years unless they came to like the slog. Sometimes it's bittersweet to reach the top, because there's nothing to do but linger for a while and then go down. This time, however, he wouldn't need to descend.

I'd started this exercise of exercising in an effort to try on a new identity, the way a high school boy might try on meanness, or a college boy might grow a goatee and expect it to change his outlook. But now, watching Dad, I realized that I'd mainly discovered what a solid thing an identity is. He, at least, was unchanged even by this catastrophe. As for me, I'd examined my core from a different side, or placed it under light of a different wavelength, and found it to be much as I'd always known it: curious, eager, tempted by deep commitment but afraid of the effort and pain. The same on a ski trail and in front of a keyboard and on my knees in church. Three-quarters of the way there in everything I did.

I could live with that—it had served me well so far—but now I wondered if I could die with that. Wondered if I could go as gracefully as my father was going, as bravely and yet as peacefully. Part of me still held out the hope of a breakthrough. Watching someone die a good death kindles certain hopes. What would it be like to reach life's end without regrets? Part of me clung to the hope that my "supreme effort," should it come, might take me somewhere new and different.

Dad took one last trip into the hospital, for one last MRI. The tumor had fired up again, the doctors said, started once more to grow. Whatever "good time" we were looking forward to had now passed. Treat him as if he was a hospice case, the doctor advised us. Don't even bother calling the ambulance if something happens—you don't want them sticking a tube down his throat. Mom listened, asked Dad if he had anything to say.

He looked up, and in a clear, conversational tone announced, "I have this fascinating vision of a white line along the edge of a riverbank."

So there's Dad, cheerful in the face of a brain tumor. And here am I, gloomy because I've caught a cold despite a winter of washing my hands more often than Lady Macbeth. Two days before the big race, and I'm reduced to obsessively waxing my skis, guzzling teas, sucking on zinc tablets, and fretting that my respiratory efficiency will be compromised.

But we rose the next morning, Sophie and Sue and I, and set out for Ottawa. There wasn't much snow along the route—in fact, there wasn't much snow anywhere. Every Nordic Web page pulsed with the same sad news: race after race canceled, as a great snow drought stretched on across the Midwest and Northeast. We were high enough up in the Adirondacks to have held a thin cover, and reportedly the Gatineau Park had a few inches as well, so the race was on. But as we drove, there was nothing but bare ground to look at. That and the mileage signs along the highway, which suddenly grabbed my attention.

One of the few blessings of metric illiteracy is that a fifty-kilometer race holds fewer terrors than, say, a thirty-five-mile race. I know how long thirty-five miles is—a long damn way. But I am an American, and on my honeymoon in Paris I once asked

an incredulous shop lady for a kilogram of Brie. So it was something of a shock to see a sign that read "Ottawa, 50 kilometers"
shortly after crossing the Canadian border. We drove for a *very*
long time. I was planning to ski this far? And eight kilometers
farther if I actually did go to Norway? It suddenly seemed highly
unlikely.

We had a big festive dinner, however, with much pasta, and
then off to an early sleep. I kept coughing and sniffling till Sue
saved the night by sticking an extra pillow under my head; after
that, I simply leaked until morning. I was up at 5:45, drank some
more water, made oatmeal in the bathroom with the teakettle,
pulled on my racing suit, and drove over to the Gatineau Park,
where the race was to begin. I was one of the first competitors to
arrive, which was good, since it meant no one else was in line at
the ski-waxing booth. I'd decided that, after everything, it was
well worth $30 to have someone else stick the right wax on as a
final coat. They patiently ironed on purple and red, and then a
coat of klister under my feet because the tracks were icy. I took
my skis outside, tried them for a few strides, and instantly felt my
mood soaring—I had rock-solid kick and lustrous glide. They felt
like perfect extensions of my legs, each twitch converted into forward momentum.

The starting pen for my wave filled with other backpack-car-
rying skiers. An official weighed the rucksacks as we came in,
making sure they topped the infant-king-Haakon line on the
scale. We shuffled back and forth in the tracks for a few minutes,
trying to stay limber, until the Norwegian ambassador to Canada
sounded the ceremonial horn and the forty of us took off.

Because of the packs, it was easy enough to keep my competition in sight, to distinguish them from the hundreds of other racers

in the other waves. Six or seven of my rivals bolted to the front, and I tried to stay in contact with them, not burning myself out but not falling so far behind that I couldn't see them. We hit the first long uphill, and almost immediately I started to gain; my legs felt so strong I had to consciously rein myself in a little, remind myself I'd be out on the course for a good three hours. One by one I picked off the guys in my wave—a fellow carrying a blaze orange knapsack, a fellow in camouflage Lycra, a fast-looking skier who somehow managed to fall on the first small downhill. Twenty minutes into the race, a fellow in a brown rucksack was in front of me, and I was pretty sure he was either second or third in my wave—in other words, if I passed him I'd be in the money. I stayed on his tail for a few minutes, pulling abreast occasionally, even chatting for a while to let him know the pace wasn't hurting me. I went a little ahead, then he passed me on a long downhill coming into a water table. I stopped for a drink and he didn't, so by the time I looked up he was a hundred yards ahead. But I didn't panic—I just resumed my old pace, and after three or four more kilometers there he was. And I passed him again.

After that I was skiing by myself, occasionally passing a slower skier from an earlier wave, but mostly having to tell myself Go Go Go. The hills just kept on coming, and my form began gradually to erode; by the halfway point I was laboring, but I knew I'd soon have some long descents to rest my muscles. I stopped for a drink of water and a ClifShot, and the people manning the table seemed concerned. "You're shivering," said one. "Are you hypothermic?" Before they could ask again, I skied off.

At some point along the course, a photographer crouched, taking pictures of everyone coming by so that he could try to sell them at the banquet that night. Through his lens, I was just one more tired-looking guy. It was an unimportant race; I was stuck somewhere in the middle of it; from the outside there was no drama at all. And yet, for me it was an epic. I crouched down in my tuck and let my muscles recover for a few minutes as the trail tilted downhill. Then came a long flat section that seemed to go on and on and on. Finally, at about forty kilometers, the trail turned back on itself, and for about five hundred yards you could see the skiers who were right behind you. Oh God—one of them had a brown backpack, the same fellow I'd passed nearly two hours before, now right on my tail, maybe forty seconds behind.

Worse, something was happening to my body. It was as if my limbs were slowing down—I couldn't make them move sharply any more, couldn't muster more than a sluggish kick. I just knew I was going to get overtaken by a brown rucksack in the last ten kilometers; I could feel myself about a give up.

And then I didn't. I made it up one hill and coasted down the other side; after that, though I was shaky below the waist and feeling absolutely drained, I managed to make myself go hard. Not fast—I was moving slowly. But fast enough, because I was still passing people. Fast enough, because every time I looked over my shoulder, the tracks were clear. You never know in cross-country skiing—the trail runs through the woods and it's full of twists and turns. People can sneak up on you. But I kept plugging, and eventually there was a sign by the trail and it said: "Finish 1000 Meters." Now I was really sorry for my metric clumsiness. Did a thousand meters mean a kilometer? Ten kilometers? My hypoxic brain fuzzed the question around for a couple of minutes without success, until suddenly the trail spit out onto an open field, and the finish was only a few hundred good old English yards away. I sprinted, I fell across the line, someone picked me up and wrapped a wool blanket around me. They said I'd come in second in my wave.

My body slowly recovered, and the adrenaline dropped, but the happiness remained. I'd told Rob I was going to make a supreme effort, and I'd made it, and if the only tangible result was that a man with a brown knapsack had not caught up to me after all, that was absolutely fine. I'd trained my body long enough to get me through those first forty kilometers, and I'd somewhere picked up enough spunk and will to get me through the last ten. I'd caught that same addictive feeling of absolute immersion in the present that I remembered from my first races the year before, but this time it was even deeper. Everything really had come together for a moment. Or perhaps a better way to say it is that everything had disappeared.

When I got back home, I tried to tell Dad about it, but it was not a good day, and I don't know whether he heard me.

# 17

Dad seemed as if he hadn't far to fall, but he did. A body is so stuffed full of life that each layer stripped away reveals another, more primordial, beneath.

He had begun to swell up. His hand was so swollen that Mom had to slide off his wedding ring, with great difficulty; he'd worn it for forty years.

More and more of the day he looked past everyone, a hundred-yard stare at the wall opposite his bed. Mom moved pictures of his granddaughters to the spot he was staring at, and he smiled.

I'd come to spend a few days, planning to head back to the Adirondacks and my family; I'd gotten into the rhythm of living in two places, three days here, three days there. Humans adapt so easily. I was nearly used to his illness, knew the aides and the time each would arrive, knew the routine for helping change him. But all of a sudden he was sliding faster; each day seemed like a logarithmic decline from the one before. Compared to his silence now, he'd been Jay Leno a month before. One night he choked on a grape; after that he lived on applesauce mixed with Decadron, and on liquids. Even those were hard to feed: Sometimes he would bite down on the straw when it went into his mouth and refuse to let go, or hold a sip of water in his mouth for five minutes, ten minutes. He wasn't being obstinate or difficult, he'd simply forgotten what you do next.

In a way, his spiraling deterioration made it easier—easier to sit there for an hour at a time and tell him how much you loved him. It wasn't the way our family usually talked, and if he'd been fully conscious it might have been too painful for him. If he'd been comatose, it might have seemed forced. But with him suspended between worlds, all of us could take turns spilling our hearts. I sang him the first songs of his alma maters, the ones he'd sung to get me to sleep as a boy: "Heaven help the foes of Washington," "The Cardinal is waving, throughout the land." And I was able to tell him stories that could not be told without crying, memories of early games of catch, of mountain climbs and beach summers, of the time when, and the time when, and the time when.

We'd been debating for weeks whether to switch his case over to hospice care, a decision not as easy as it sounds. Such a switch would mean acknowledging how close the end had come, but it also had a practical side. In this era of medical limits, it would mean less help, not more, two hours of visits from the aides each day instead of four. As the week wore on, though, the aides grew less and less useful; there was no longer any hope of getting him out of bed. And we began to worry that it his heart stopped, some nurse would try to save him, poke a tube down his throat or pound on his chest.

By Saturday, he was clearly starting to feel some pain. I was holding his hand as we listened to Gerry Mulligan on the CD player, and every few minutes he would grit his teeth so hard I was sure he'd break them. Mom decided it was finally the moment to call in the hospice team, but it turned out, when we phoned, that we'd need to wait until 9 a.m. on Monday to even talk to the caseworker. And so we just kept our vigil, trying to feed him his meds, trying to keep him comfortable. His spasms were timed like pains in early labor—every six or seven minutes he'd go rigid, and all the attention in the room would focus on him, and then he'd relax, and we'd relax.

Oh, and of course I would still go out for runs, for quick skis in the gerbil wheel. Nothing else calmed me at all—not sleep, certainly. But the irony of strapping on my heart rate monitor and keeping careful track of my beats while Dad's heart was laboring simply to keep going was not lost on me either. I'd spent so much of the year working on endurance, and now it was being tested in some real way, and often I felt as if I was failing. I'd sit next to Dad, and when I was done crying, then I'd want some distraction. It was great joy to simply have the chance to stare at his face, not a chance you get too often with anyone save your children and your spouse. But it was so intense, the realization that he was leaving. I found I couldn't think about it hour after hour. This supreme effort was beyond me—I'd pick up the newspaper, turn on the radio. "Sit with me this hour"—but my spirit and my flesh were both weak.

By Monday, his hands were curling into claws, his body contracting back toward some fetal grace. The bag at the end of his catheter tube was now filling slowly with dark orange urine. His body was shutting down, piece by piece. All the things it had done forever, it kept doing, but barely, like a racer running on pure instinct at the end of a marathon. He was hitting the wall, bonking—his kidneys and his liver kept at their work, the same work they'd been doing since before he was even born, but they were operating only on momentum now. He was winding down.

By Tuesday, when the hospice nurse finally arrived to take over, only the stare survived. We got his steroid pills down him one last time that morning, but it was clear that would be the end of it, that his brain would now be free to swell as it wanted to. He might die by evening, the nurse said, and so everyone was summoned.

But he didn't die. He got more agitated instead, breathing rough and hard and ragged, a horrible sound that made us sure he was in pain. Tom and I called the hospice hotline; they found a pharmacist who would open his shop. At midnight we were in downtown Boston, scoring a bottle of morphine from a darkened drugstore.

It didn't help much at first. We gave him a dose under the tongue and started taking shifts with him. He would breathe hard four or five times, and then he would cease for a few seconds. Those few seconds seemed to get longer and longer; surely, soon, he would forget to start up again and it would all be over. In fact, when the nurse came back, she said he was "actively dying." But the morphine eventually had its effect, and his breathing began to relax. As morning wore on into afternoon into evening, he calmed. We sat with him, talking and joking over his sleeping form; Mom went once more through the scrapbook of the years they'd spent in England ("Here's the house on Jubilee Lane, do you remember those lovely roses?"), talking as if he could hear her, and perhaps he could.

The periods between breaths kept stretching out, though—long periods of apnea, ten or twelve seconds when he was floating, like a toy balloon racing up toward the sky, only to be brought up short by its string. Dad's sister, Helena, who'd spent her life as a doctor, was there, and she timed the gaps on her wristwatch. "It won't be long now," she said, but it was.

As dark started to fall, Tom went out for a short walk, and I took the dog into the backyard. We'd just gotten back into the bedroom when he opened his eyes for the first time all day, lurched forward, and stopped breathing.

And there were tears left in us, it turned out, lots of them. We fell across his bed, across his body, and sobbed a lot of things, some of them incoherent, most of them "Thank you, thank you, thank you." His body cooled fairly fast, and his lips pulled back—his teeth were bared, he looked almost as if he was snarling. But Mom said, "Oh what a beautiful body," and each in our own way, with our own memories, agreed. Not beautiful because he had made of it a project or a task, but because it had been the physical form that made his goodness real. That gave it a shape—lanky, bald—that lasted into memory. Beautiful for all it had contained.

The undertaker arrived, and wheeled him down that carefully built wheelchair ramp to take him to the crematorium, and his race was over.


Except that the minute a race is done, you start trying to make it all add up, turn the thousand things that happen even in a three-hour ski into some kind of coherent story with a moral at the end: "I couldn't focus," or "I bonked," or "Everything came together."

You need the story, simplified and reduced as it necessarily is, if you want to hold on to the race; otherwise, it slips back into ever-dimming memory.

So we collected pictures from the basement—Dad in his christening dress, Dad in high school, Dad at his wedding looking impossibly young, Dad as a cub reporter, Dad as a dad. We gathered the documentary evidence: the bound volumes of the *Stanford Daily,* which he'd edited in college; the stacks of articles from the *Wall Street Journal* and *Business Week* and the *Boston Globe*; copies of his book. And we winnowed through our memories, trying to write eulogies that would make some shape of his life.

My brother, Tom, talked about his enthusiasm and his lack of pretension. Ron Ostrow, his best friend, talked about his steadfastness. Steve Bailey, a colleague at the *Globe*, talked about his sheer decency as an editor and a boss. Dan Smith, his minister, described all the volunteer work he'd done. And I said what I could think of to say, which had everything to do with this endless year of sweating, and the attempt to figure out what it meant to be a man, and the example that had been under my nose the whole time:

> He was a truly remarkable man, in large measure because he didn't think of himself as remarkable. In fact, he seemed to think of himself very little. There was a kind of egolessness about him that seems as wonderful to me as it seems unlikely. In a profession and an age dominated by ego, he thought very little about his career, his glory, his future, what he wanted to do right now. He cared about his work, of course—cared about it enormously, and did it to a high standard. But he never let it get in the way of his relations with other people—with colleagues of every level and stripe, with friends and family, especially with his wife . . .. His marriage was the supreme

work of art in his life, more lovely and permanent than even his book or his best pieces of writing. For as long as I can remember, he and Mom truly engaged in the work of being married—truly tried to put the other one first, until it was almost second nature.

In his last few weeks, he had visions of a river, of an ocean. He was, I feel certain, becoming more and more confident that he would once again find himself in the forests and high mountains that he had known as a boy and loved all his life. But wonderful as those visions were, they belonged to his future. In his present, right until the very end, he was the same man that he had been for decades. The last real conversation I had with him came just last weekend. He hadn't really talked for several days, but I was just sitting by his bed, chatting almost. I said, "Mom is really doing great, you know, even better than I thought she would."

And he looked at me and said clearly and forcefully, "She is, isn't she?"

And then I said that we all—family and friends—would help care for her when he was gone. And he simply said, "Good. Good." And that was that.

His example, frankly, is intimidating. Sue and I have been married eleven years now, and I've come nowhere near the state of grace he seemed to come by effortlessly. But what a gift it was that he gave us, this understanding that you could be a man his way, full of love and kindness and good humor and hard work. But not full of yourself.

Home from church to friends, and flowers, and beer; home to clean out the sickroom and return the hospital bed and stow the pictures and the momentos.

Though Dad's sickness had lasted barely six months, half the impossibly short "average life expectancy" the doctors had given us at the start, the profiles of those months seemed as jagged and unpredictable as the profiles of the racecourses I would download off my computer. I'd spent the first couple of months half convinced we should shut Dad down, half hoping that something would kill him fast. More than half hoping. I didn't like watching, and I didn't like feeling compelled to watch. It would have been easier for everyone if he'd just died.

But he'd endured. He'd kept going. He'd done his work, begun the transition to whatever came after, figured out about the ocean he was aiming for, all the while keeping his personality intact.

And he'd made the rest of us endure, too, do some of our work. My mother, always pacific even to a fault, had come into her own. With the center of her life incapacitated, she had become as aggressive and powerful as the situation demanded. A few nights before Dad died, one of the more hapless aides had, for the umpteenth time, nearly dumped him out of bed. Mom looked up at this giant fellow and said, "If you ever do that again I'm going to punch you in the mouth," a remark for which she instantly felt sorry, but which left the rest of us giggling—and fully confident that she'd be able to take care of herself in the years to come.

I'd spent the year thinking about endurance. Trying to understand it as a function of physiology, of lactic acid and capillary networks. Trying to understand it as the ability to fight through the drama of pain. But now I understand it, too, as a kind of elegance, a lightness that could come only from such deep comfort with yourself that you began to forget about yourself. Something from the heart that no monitor would ever measure.

Dad's last gift had been to snap me out of my self-absorption. Like Rob, like Easwaran the Marin guru, like Grandmother Rainbow for all I know, he understood that a certain grace descended on those who forgot themselves. He *was* in balance. A powerful man. Perhaps we'd had our good time after all.

# 18

If you want to understand cross-country skiing in Norway, let me describe an evening I spent once in Oslo. Dinner was artic char baked in sesame seeds, followed by filet of reindeer in lingonberry sauce. Out the front door of the hotel, a woman I'd met a day before was waiting—tall and striking, Liv Arnesen was the first woman to ski solo to the South Pole. We snapped on our skis and set off on the lighted double tracks; soon we were deep in the woods, alone, flying along between endless spruces. Every once in a while a high ridge would show us the city spread out in lights below, and then another whistling plunge into the woods—it was crisp, silent skiing, very nearly like a dream.

The tracks led us back to town, finally—to the Holmenkollen, site of the mammoth ski jump and spiritual center of Nordic skiing. A floodlight shone on the statue of the late King Olav, who jumped off the big hill when he was in his twenties. But the statue shows him at age eighty, clad in an anorak, skiing with his poodle. King and dog would ride up on the streetcar from the palace many afternoons, and then ski off into the woods.

On a knoll above the statue, we could hear music coming from the Holmenkollen chapel. Inside, in a sanctuary of carved wood all lit with candles, the Oslo Chamber Choir sang Norwegian folk hymns. Sang them angelically, to an audience whose skis were stacked by the door.

I'd come to Norway to ski the Birkebeiner—Dad had thoughtfully perished with enough time left for Sue and Sophie and me to book tickets. Once I thought this would be the epic end of my tale. But I'd already had what epiphanies the year would produce—perhaps in the last few kilometers of that race in Ottawa, certainly late in the night by the rasping side of my father.

Still, to write about endurance without visiting Norway (or Kenya) would be wrong. It is a place defined in some ways by endurance. Oslo, a city of half a million, has 2,600 kilometers of groomed, tracked ski trails a ten-minute tram ride from the center of town. Every kindergarten in Oslo has a ski day every week all winter. Every taxi in Oslo has a ski rack. Why? Not simply because it's cold and snowy—it's cold and snowy in Buffalo, too, a city of about the same size, which is famous for a certain kind of chicken wing dipped in blue cheese dressing.

No, the answers lie deep in Norwegian history, so deep that you have to come inside and take a shower and sit down with a glass of Ringnes beer and with Tor Bamann-Larsen, the author of a book whose title translates, more or less, as "The Everlasting Snow: An Ideology of Skiing." Tor may be the planet's only ski intellectual; his latest book is a massive biography of Roald

Amundsen, who planted Norway's flag at the South Pole. And he's eager to talk.

Though skiing is an ancient Nordic means of transport—there's a pair of skis in the national museum that are four thousand years old—its modern incarnation as a sport really began in 1867 and 1868 when a group of farmers from the town of Telemark came down to the capital to give a ski show. They jumped, they slalomed, they—they telemarked. And they took the city by storm. "It became nearly a religion for the leading people of Oslo—the officers, the lawyers," said Tor. "You learned to be a Norwegian *here*," he added, pointing at his brow. "And *here*," pointing to his heel.

Norway had long languished under the dominion of the Danes or the Swedes, but as in Germany and Italy and much of the rest of Europe, its national blood was starting to stir in the late nineteenth century. Norwegian writers began to evoke the Viking past. And Fridtjof Nansen, who was born in Oslo and learned to ski from the Telemarkers, began to evoke a new Viking future. He skied across Greenland, the first man to do so, and came home to incredible fanfare. "It was the first time in modern history that Norway had made something in the world. We saw that we could be like the Vikings, only this time we would do it on skis," said Tor. The North Pole, the South Pole (while Scott trudged, Amundsen skied), the Northwest Passage—after each conquest great parades and torchlight rallies surged through the streets of Oslo.

In 1905, like some skinny teenager redeemed by a few years with free weights, Norway finally felt strong enough to strike out on its own. Nansen went to Denmark and recruited a prince to serve as Norway's new king—and one of the very first things he taught King Haakon, formerly a sea officer, was how to ski.

To be a Norwegian *means* to ski—a pair of Fischers means to a Norwegian what a set of car keys means to a suburban American child. Not just freedom—*identity*. And to be a Norwegian means to ski a particular code, which Tor explained: "To be out in nature is the most important thing."

"And you have to ski up as well as down."

Which explains why the small town of Lillehammer, site of the 1994 Olympics, was packed by the time we arrived in mid-March. Birkebeiner organizers were expecting over 9,000 skiers for the big Saturday race; given Norway's population of just over 4 million, that's the equivalent of, oh, 650,000 people showing up for the start of the Boston Marathon. And it's not even the biggest race in Norway—a slightly less grueling Oslo-area tour draws 15,000 annually.

Lillehammer somehow avoided being wrecked by the Olympics. Its main shopping streets are left unplowed all winter so that shoppers can schuss their groceries home on sleds. They stand on a runner on the back and kick as you would a scooter. Currier and Ives would drool.

The biggest business in town seemed to be the Swix factory, where great vats of blue and green and red ski wax are poured into little tins and shipped to cross-country skiers in every latitude. Norwegians tour in the way Americans might visit a brewery. Inside the front door there's a wax museum, with tins dating back a century. "They used anything for wax in those days," said factory chief Harald Bjerke. "They'd melt down pine resin, butter, bicycle tires. When vinyl records came in, they'd melt those."

Now it's high science, with fluorinated compounds so toxic that waxers wear special gas masks; Bjerke loaded me down with papers on the "Tribophysics of Skiing" ("The low coefficient of kinematic friction found in the system is partly explained by thin-water films") and free samples, and then sent me off to meet Rolf Kjoernsli, seventy-five, who has skied the Birkebeiner forty-four times and would tackle it for the forty-fifth on Saturday.

Kjoernsli's English was perfect—he did a stint at Oxford after the war, his reward for his work as a demolitions expert for the Resistance. He told me about one of his most memorable races, just a few years earlier, when he'd needed to have a hip replaced, but decided to wait until after the Birkie. "I skied together with my surgeon the last few kilometers, and in the shower afterwards we were sharing a bit of schnapps. He wanted to have one more, but I said, 'It's me you're operating on tomorrow.' The hip doesn't function as well as in the old days, but I'm still upright." Though Kyoernsli had been an elite ski racer in his day, coaching Olympic squads, he said most of the Birkebeiner skiers raced only once a winter. "People train for it all year. It's their exam, their annual test of willpower and stamina."

I'd see them practicing whenever I went to the Olympic ski stadium for my own final workouts. Perfect form, even the slow ones. That was less intimidating than the soft, soggy snow, though. The whole week before the race, the temperature hovered around a drizzling, dreary zero—precisely the hardest conditions to wax for. And so the thought of fifty-eight kilometers uphill, with no kick, began to haunt me. Against my will, contrary to the calm I was trying to cultivate, I began to scurry around in the same panicky sweat that had marked my very first race fifteen months before. What wax? What wax?

Me and everyone else, as it turned out. Swix started issuing daily bulletins advising skiers exactly what to put on the bottom of their skis. People lined up outside sporting goods shops to get expert advice. One store even agreed to wax my skis, but when I went to pick them up the next day it turned out that the owner's wife had had a baby and that was that. Anyway, conditions were changing too fast to predict. On Friday night I jumped aboard the bus to Rena, where the race would begin, clutching my sleeping bag and my unwaxed skis.

Lillehammer had seemed like a normal resort town with a bunch of skiers passing through; the night before the Birkeh-beiner, however, Rena was like no place I'd ever seen. Every public building had been converted into a dormitory. I was shown to a mattress on the third floor of a trade school, where I pitched my gear and went out for a walk. All over Rena, extension cords dangled out of windows, powering irons for the waxing gangs that gathered everywhere. All anyone could talk about was wax—how cold would it be, how humid? (In the technical papers Bjerke had given me at the waxworks the day before, I found the following encouraging footnote: "There is no material of engineering significance that displays the bewildering complexities of snow.") Swix had stationed weather forecasters several hundred kilometers out at sea to radio in the latest conditions, by seven o'clock on Friday night, posters all over town were urging people to rub on four layers of extra blue, and then cork in xf40 and xf50, a pair of expensive, little-used waxes. I did, and I went to sleep, and I got up three times to pee just as I was supposed to, and finally all the snoring stopped and morning came.

Out at the start, thousands upon thousands of skiers milled aggressively around, trying to stay warm. Swix had set up dozens of waxing tables, and their technicians were still repeating the same advice. I skied a practice loop, slipping at every stride, and I started to sweat in panic. I knew that there was no way I could climb all those hills slipping like this. Suddenly, despite all my training, I started to feel like an impostor again—all those other people milling around in Lycra looked like the *real* skiers. I grew timid in my own judgment. Surely, I kept telling myself, the Swix technicians must know what they are up to—we were only a few miles from company headquarters, after all.

Finally the bell rang for us thirty-five- to forty-year-olds, and we surged across the line. And right from the start I knew I'd made a mistake not listening to my gut. I was spinning my wheels like a car caught in a snowbank, trying desperately to find the traction that would get me up the hills. I kept going like that for ten minutes, hoping that as I got higher the snow would change. But it didn't, and so like hundreds of other skiers I had to take my skis off, pull new wax out of my pocket, and watch hopelessly as the smarter skiers powered by.

By the time I was back on the course, I knew my chances for a fast time were gone. And your chances for a *good* time are pretty low, too, when you're gasping uphill hour after hour. But if I wasn't racing at my flat-out best, I didn't snap into some other world either, didn't psych myself out. Adrenaline swept me up the first 15K of hills, till we emerged on a barren windswept plateau. Two mountains still loomed ahead—shorter climbs, but by then my legs were tiring. There was no one to race—or, rather, there were so many thousands of other skiers that I couldn't pick one out and stick to his heels, work myself into a frenzy. So I went deep inside, kept track of my weakening calves and my tightening chest, measured my resources against the distance left to go.

Every so often I'd go past one of the skiers who had started earlier, some of them men much older than Kjoernsli. I'd met a ninety-two-year-old in Oslo, one of the first men to ski across Greenland. "He's a little shaky when he's walking across the parking lot," a friend had said, "but once he clicks into his skis, he's fine." It was easy to imagine these old men a half century before, skiing silently out to meet the Allied airdrops deep in the woods. They'd endured, made a grand quiet passion out of enduring. They and all the other thousands of people streaming down the trail—whenever I reached a straight stretch, I'd look ahead and it was as crowded as Fifth Avenue at lunch hour. Instead of individual triumph, a kind of collective glory hovered over the tracks.

And it all came out just fine—a little over four hours of hard skiing, ending with a series of sharp downhills into the Olympic stadium, where brass bands and cheering crowds greeted us. I finished just above the middle of my age group, which I declared a great victory, considering they were all Norwegians. But I took my conquest as quietly as everyone else—there was no whooping or hollering on the bus to the showers, just satisfied and tired smiles. The year was over, and it was time for a smoked salmon pizza and a bottle of Ringnes and some Tiger Balm to rub on my aching thighs.

And the next morning dawned clear and cold, so Sue and Sophie and I went for another ski. For the first time in a long time, it meant nothing at all, and that was nice too.

# Afterword

I remembered visiting Boulder, Colorado, the first time. For an endurance athlete, it's a kind of theme park. Packs of Kenyans and Ethiopians lope the trails around town, training full-time in the thin altitude and the Front Range splendor. Sneaker stores abound, each one with an old Olympian or two behind the counter, dispensing advice. Studly triathletes on their new titanium-frame bikes crowd the roads into the mountains. Everyone—*everyone*—wears Oakleys. "Being a full-time athlete is a perfectly acceptable occupation—no one looks at you funny," Ray Browning, the ironman champion and longtime Boulderite says. "The biggest psychological problem in town, though, is people who can't retire, who can't figure out what their identity is going to be when their career is over, or how they're supposed to spend their days when they're not on a training schedule."

As usual, I had just a smidgen of a sense of what he was talking about. I hadn't spent my whole life in training, but training had been most of my life for more than a year, and it was hard to figure out how to slack off.

Part of the withdrawal was purely physical. Some months after our Norwegian trip, I traveled again, this time to Bangladesh. I was there to report on climate change, on how global warming is triggering massive floods that threaten the very integrity of a beautiful and sweet-tempered nation. I interviewed dozens of people, toured the countryside, found myself completely fascinated—and also slipped into severe exercise deprivation. It wasn't simply that I was too busy to work out; it was almost physically impossible. Never mind the 90 degree heat and 90 percent humidity. Bangladesh is a crowded place: 140 million people squeezed into an area the size of Wisconsin. What that means is no empty roads, no empty sidewalks, few empty parks. Even way out in the countryside, the cart tracks are filled with processions of people on bicycles, people on foot, people clinging to tilting buses. People haul timber one or two logs at a time on pushcarts, and pedal-powered rickshaws jangle past constantly. "Why do you think we don't have good soccer teams?" one man asked me. "No room for a proper pitch." The only running tracks I saw were on military bases, surrounded with barbed wire.

And so, after about a week without any real movement at all, my body began to rebel: My legs were cramping, my back aching. If I stepped on and off my bed five hundred times, sweating in air that a ceiling fan tried bootlessly to cool, I could ease the pain and go to sleep. I hadn't had a beer in weeks—they're hard to find in Muslim Bangladesh—but I was glad to see that it wasn't much of an addiction, at least compared to exercise. My dreams of home had mainly to do with long, empty trails just waiting for a runner. (Before I could get on them I had to wait out the dengue fever that I contracted in my last few days in Dhaka—but that's another story.)

If my calves were cramping those first few months, though, my mind was hurting more. Most of the withdrawal pains were purely psychological; as my fitness started to ebb a little, so did my identity. It's true that I'd never been a *real* athlete, in the sense that my prowess defined me. Even when I was ski racing, I was a *writer* ski racing. Still, being in killer shape had begun to inform my sense of who I was, the picture of me that I carried around in my head. I'd enjoyed mightily thinking of myself as a bit of a powerhouse, lean and tough. That VO2 Max, built on hundreds of hours of training, was like money in the bank, and if that training stopped, the money would begin to drain away, eroded by the inflation (literal and metaphorical) of normal life. I was extremely conscious of the fact that I was now nearly forty, an age when it seemed as if it would be harder to start all over again if I so desired. Consequently, I was as scared as a miser of losing my hoard. Not only that, but all of a sudden I actually had to *do* things to justify my days. Had to write articles, give speeches, do my real work. I couldn't simply cross off another day's mileage and consider myself morally excused.

And so Rob and I worked out a new program, about 350 hours a year of exercise, roughly half of what I'd been doing. It was still a lot, in comparison with the average American's more or less sedentary way of life. It was still a lot by almost any measure, in fact. But to me it seemed almost trivial, a breeze. The longest runs were two hours. *Two hours! That's all!* When my wife and I were first married, we'd lived in Manhattan, and for the next fifteen years, no matter where we were, life seemed inexpensive compared to the Upper West Side. The same with this Regimen Lite. A good thing, too, because we moved to Boston for a couple of years to be near my mom, and so, suddenly, I found myself running not in the mountains but along the Charles River. A classic place to run, but . . . kind of flat. Extraordinarily flat, in fact—I found myself looking forward to places where small *mounds* meant five steps off the horizontal. Kind of dull after a while. Impossible without the radio for diversion. In the winter, skiing meant the endless golf course gerbil wheel. If my heart rate monitor could have detected emotional interest, it would have shown a flat line.

Still, there were races to look forward to, a few weekends each winter to journey back into the mountains and look for that sweet spot, that zone of desperate concentration that had begun to seem almost familiar. And what do you know—eighteen months after I finished my die-hard training, I finally won a race. That is to say, I won my age group in a race. With a pretty thin field. *But still . . . .*

It happened in Lake Placid, on the old Olympic trails at Mt. Van Hoevenberg, during the classic old-time winter of 2000-2001. Snow was falling and the temperature was climbing—touch waxing territory, but Chris Seymour, who had coached junior skiers at Van Ho for a decade, offered to wax my skis. We were still tinkering ten minutes before the gun went off ("I'm slipping—get me some klister"), but when I ran to the start line with thirty seconds to go, I knew I had fast skis. And as it turned out, I had reasonably fast legs as well, at least that day. The course wound up one incline after another, peaking at Russian Hill, so named because the Soviets complained long and hard about its slope during the Games. That climb came about halfway through the twenty-five kilometers, and after that, as the trail turned flatter, I simply held on. My body felt strangely strong, stronger in some ways than during my most serious training. Which makes a certain amount of sense: I may not have been building myself up quite as much, but I wasn't tearing myself down as assiduously either. Training is a kind of violence, and reducing it, at least in the short run, leaves you stronger. My aerobic base still served me pretty well, and I had energy to burn.

Strange too was the fleeting feeling of satisfaction that came with victory. I had assumed, I think, that the enterprise looked different from the top step of the podium, and perhaps it does if you visit there regularly. But if it *really* did, then champions would retire early instead of hanging on too long. My elation wore off in a day or two; mainly, I think, I was relieved that I had done well enough to have some mental excuse to keep training even at my reduced rate for another summer.

Glory of all sorts wears off quickly—by afternoon the morning's fine book review has receded toward the back of your mind. So you've either got to arrange for regular triumphs or learn to enjoy instead the long slog that keeps you in the game.

Other things wear off as well. At the moment my father died, it seemed impossible that the emotional power of that moment, the overwhelming sense of life's fragility and urgency and beauty, would simply erode. But of course it did—that's how we're built. I missed him, sometimes acutely, but he was vanishing into that hazy, slightly idealized world where people go when they die. I didn't want the lessons he'd taught me to go with him.

Most of the long chain of gurus, cranks, and messiah that have illumined human civilization have agreed on one point: that it's what you do every day, day in day out, that forms who you are. Not what you do on special occasions. Clearly this was true of one's physical life: You could go out tomorrow and force yourself to run ten miles, and if it was the only run you did all month, your body would not change at all (except that it would be very stiff and sore for a few days). It's the long accretion of elevated heartbeats, of muscle-fiber twitches, of deep breaths that over time remake your plumbing, resize your lungs. And I knew from even longer experience that the same held true for intellectual life. Sudden flashes of insight might propel you forward, but those sudden flashes only came to people who worked with consistent dedication to learn the new, to master the old.

What Dad's death taught me, I think, was that the same holds true for the spiritual life, to use a grander term than he would ever have employed. People's deaths often really do magnify who they are, intensify their essence instead of disguising it. His serenity and grace and egolessness were not sudden saintly touches applied with strenuous effort at the very end; they were the grooves into which his life had fallen by long practice of kindness and selflessness. Not in any dramatic way (or in his case perhaps any conscious way), but instead in the simple daily encounter with those around him. That patient, unflashy drip drip drip of love changed him as fundamentally as (more fundamentally than) my patient daily drop of long slow runs. Occasionally real tests arise, times when you need to consciously and maybe painfully lay aside something you want to do in order for your spouse or your child to find their fulfillment—call those uphill intervals, wind sprints. You don't want to do them, but you're stronger because of them. And then there are the longer tests, more like marathons: sickness, depression, all the flavors of angst and ennui, all the sad temptations of hypermaterialism and hyperindividualism. They are like races, I suppose, calling for all the strength that daily habit has engraved in your heart. The most profound test, of course, is the last one, dealing with your death. But if you've done the training, the race will take care of itself—or so it seemed, watching Dad.

This metaphor is too grand, doubtless. Life as an endurance race. But what made this project so sweet for me was the dawning understanding that an endurance race, though tough, was also enormous fun. Even though it didn't supply any of the things—comfort, convenience, security—that our society trains us to want, it provides much deeper joy. As does, I suspect, a committed life of the mind or of the heart. At any rate, I'd like to find out. Right now, though, it's time for my run.

# ACKNOWLEDGMENTS FROM THE FIRST EDITION

I could not have attempted this odd project of mine, nor written this book, without the help of an extraordinary number of people. A few of them are identified in the book, but many more are not. Let me say thanks, first, to Rob Sleamaker, my coach, who was unfailingly positive and grew into a dear friend. Those who want specific guidelines for long-distance training could do no better than buy the classic book he co-wrote with Ray Browning, *Serious Training for Endurance Athletes.* (And those who want specific exercises for cross-country skiers should seek out the superb *Fitness Cross-Country Skiing* by Steve Gaskill.) People from all around the world of cross-country skiing lent me equipment and advice: John Schweizer and Tom Rogers at Peltonen, Steve Poulin at Swix, Steve Quinaug at Alpina, Jim Fredericks at Rossignol, Andrew Gerlach and his friends at Salomon and Fischer, who also let me work out with their Factory Team, including Kathryn Strickland, John Yarrington, and Clark Sullivan. John Brodhead and the staff of the Craftsbury Outdoor Center not only let me ski, they also taught me a great deal, as did the editors of *The Master Skier, Cross-Country Skier,* fasterskier.com, *Trax,* and *Runner's World,* and Brian Delaney at High Peaks Cyclery. I'm also extremely grateful to John Underwood, to Tracy Lamb, Ken Rundell, and the other staff of the Olympic Training Center at Lake Placid, to Ben Husaby and his teammates, to Eknath Easwaran and the residents of the Blue Mountain Center, to Phil and Rene Rumpff, to the staffs of the Kripalu Center and the Salmon Hills Ski Center. Len Johnson and Torbjörn Karlsen were helpful with equipment and advice. And I was inspired not only by the Factory Team skiers I describe—Husaby, Carl Swenson, Erich Wilbrecht, Nathan Schultz, Pete Vordenberg, Trond Nystrad, Laura McCabe, and others—but also by the best American skiers of our time, whom I got to watch (and even, in my fashion, race against): Marc Gilbertson, Patrick Weaver, John Bauer, Marcus Nash, Kris Freeman, Justin Wadsworth, Cory Smith, Nina Kemppel, and many many more. And, of course, Björn.

I skied on three continents and at dozens and dozens of different areas, but I never found one to match my skiing home—the Garnet Hill Ski Center in North River, New York—for variety of terrain, loveliness of scenery, and quality of grooming. Many thanks to Dick Carlson, who oversees it all; George Heim, who owns it all; and the many folk who make it work: Jeff Fosdick, Richard Stewart, Greg Chudowsky, Bo Columbine, J. R. Pratt, Joel Beaudin, Julie Stanistreet, Doug Cole, Kate Bayse, Scott Pavlacovic, Chris Moon, Martin Olsen, Marko and Amelia Schmale, Josie Fosdick, Larry Wilke, and Art Perryman. My friends and skiing buddies in the Adirondacks all made life much sweeter: Nick and Jackie Avignon, Gary and Kathy Wilson, Mike Dabroski and Lisa Spilde, Mitch Hay and Barb Lemmel, Jonathan Rubinstein and Linda Motzkin, Russell Puschak and Kate Gardner, Jack and Tim Burke, Jim Gould, Pete Gilbertson and Ellen Dupree, Amanda Smith-Socaris, Sam and Susan Allison, Dick and Dee Warner, Jenna Stauffer, Steve Sexton, Martha Sandsted, Joe Kahn, John Elder, Doug Diehl, Mike Wynn, Jim Tucker, and Nancie Battaglia, Kelly Rose, and Kris Seymour. Sam and Lisa Verhovek and Shawn and Michael Considine were, as usual, instrumental.

An enormous number of people, including many of the friends listed, helped our family in the long months when my father was dying. The medical personnel included Dr. Edmund B. Goldman, Dr. Philip Steig, Dr. Timothy Shafman, Dr. Arthur Sasahara, Rachel Silverman, R.N., and—first and foremost—Sarajune Degan, R.N., whose efforts were truly above and beyond the call. The nurses and aides of the ICU and oncology floors at Brigham and Women's Hospital were wonderful, as were the staff of the New England Rehabilitation Hospital, including Dr. Denise Ozell, Sherri McDonough, Jocelyn Leger, and Tanya Tammaro, Laurie Austin, Brian King, and the nurses and aides of the N2 wing. The Mt. Auburn Home Care visiting nurses included Alicia Whitney Mici, Kate Horn, and Mary Jane Jacobs. The aides, whose good humor and tender care in a difficult situation will be long remembered, included Gabriel Lorius, Faveur Beauchamps, Alicia Kowalska, Marie Donnelly, Lynn Singh, Pat Mullins, Yanra Sanches, Bill Murphy, and Joyce Henry. Private evening aides included Annette Kalisa, Donna Lord, and Pellissier Andre. Physical therapist Patty Andrews and speech therapist Jerry Kaplan brought cheer and laughter, as well as their technical skills. Harvard Pilgrim healthcare social workers Amy Cohen and Amy Bogan and their staff were helpful in coordinating the intricacies of HMO care. And the employees of Health Care Dimensions, a hospice care agency, performed their difficult jobs with skill and compassion: Linda Powell, Julie Lee, Deborah Sherman Hayes, and Judith Oliver.

A family trying to cope with such crushing changes requires more than medical help. We benefited greatly from the succor of friends:

the diaconate and staff of Hancock United Church of Christ (the Reverend Dan Smith, who served as my parents' main spiritual counselor, the Reverend Peter Meek, the Reverend Gay Godfrey, and Karen Coope) as well as a wide array of church members and local friends. First among them, Cynthia and Charles Calvin, their son Keith, and all the other members of their family, as well as Faith and Jim Fenske, Connie Devereux, Isabel and Horace Besecker, Ruth and Bob Sawyer, Tom and Betty Taylor, Frank and Carol Caro, Peggy and Bob Bicknell, Louise and Bruce Rankin, Marcia and Ken Bushnell, Jim and Lois Gallagher, Phyllis Nygard, Ed and Myrtle Cox, Bob Foster, Nancy and Bob Earsy, Dorothy Martin and her son, Stephan, Ceci and Ben Potter, Priscilla and Bruce Kinney, Pat and Phil Hadley, Marian and Kay Barney, Ruth and Sam Nablo, Faith and Alton Armington, Marge and Jack Wyman, Justine and John Federici, Jim Jones and Debbie Beers, Cindy and Tom Stander, Jane and Jim Buckley, Lucy Short, John Short, and many friends from local organizations like P.E.O., FISH, and the Bicentennial Band, whose flute section played "Ode to Joy" at my father's funeral.

My father's family—Ernie and Ardis McKibben, Betty and Bill McKibben, and Helena Kirkwood; my cousins Craig, Connie, Margaret, Barry, Andy, Barbara, and Kathy and all their families; Ben, Helen, Will, and Suzi Hayes and their families; and friends like Ron and Alyce Ostrow, Pat Ostrow, Rick and Ying Ying Brown, Donna Moore, Jane and Peter Gharibian, Lynnette Cawthra and Mike Chambers, the Reverend Malcolm and Sylvia Braddy, all provided crucial assistance and warm memories, as did my father's old colleagues at the *Boston Globe:* Tom Winship, Steve Bailey, Jack Driscoll, Mary O'Rourke, Charles Stein, Jerry Ackerman, Bill Davis, Chris Tree, and Paul Hemp. Other old friends also made the hard days easier, and often joyful: Bob and Diane Batlin, Art and Sue Lempert, Dorothy Dodge, Jean McDonald, Sue Cony, Art Abrams, Dave and Marty Wilson, Joanie Kilgore, Peter and Harriet Shoup, Betty and Hal Watkins, Jeanne and Fred Henry, Boyard and Anne Rowe, Bob and Nancy Sievert, Hildy Soule, Dick Cress, Margaret and Seig Lindstorm, Ray and Claire Lincoln, Pat and Dave Hallin, Eileen and Jerry Lehmer, Doug and Rita Locker, Virginia and Wade Sherwood, Charles Morgan, Esther Tye Smith, Suzanne John, Beth Levine, Bob Hilton, Jayne Gordon, Judy Pippin, David and Helen Jones, Russ Coberly, David and Doris Fausch, Joan Gallagher, Lisa and John Barstow, and Steve and Lisa Braydon.

My brother, Tom, his wife, Kristy, and their daughter Ellie gave Dad more support than anyone else except, of course, my mother. I can barely begin to describe her courage, and the inspiration of her example.

This book itself took shape under the wise eyes of my editors, David Rosenthal and Geoff Kloske, and all their colleagues at Simon & Schuster, including Annik LaForge, Zoë Wolff, Nicole Graev, Aileen Boyle, Amanda Wilkins, Stephen Messina, and Victoria Meyer. As usual, my agent Gloria Loomis provided immense help and encouragement, and I'm grateful as well to her assistant, Katherine Fausset. Hal Espen and his staff at *Outside* understood the idea early on and offered valuable aid.

And then there were Sue and Sophie. I kept their pictures with me when I raced, but it was hardly necessary, for they are always in my heart.

# ABOUT THE AUTHOR

BILL MCKIBBEN is the author of *The End of Nature* and a dozen other books, mostly about the environment. In 2010, the *Boston Globe* called him "probably America's leading environmentalist," and *Time* said he was "the planet's best green journalist." A former staff writer for the *New Yorker*, his work has also appeared in *Outside, Rolling Stone,* the *New York Review of Books, Harper's* and the *Atlantic Monthly.* He was founder of 350.org, the largest grassroots climate campaign in the planet's history. He lives in the Green Mountains of Vermont.